The Civilian Conservation Corps in Nevada

Wilbur S. Shepperson Series in Nevada History
Series Editor Michael Green

The Civilian Conservation Corps in Nevada
From Boys to Men

Renée Corona Kolvet and Victoria Ford

Foreword by Richard O. Davies

University of Nevada Press Reno & Las Vegas

This book is made possible in part by a grant from Nevada Humanities, a state program of the National Endowment for the Humanities.

University of Nevada Press, Reno, Nevada 89557 USA

Manufactured in the United States of America

Design by Omega Clay

Library of Congress Cataloging-in-Publication Data
Kolvet, Renée Corona.
The Civilian Conservation Corps in Nevada : from boys to men / Renée Corona Kolvet and Victoria Ford ; foreword by Richard O. Davies.
p. cm. — (Wilbur S. Shepperson series in Nevada history)
Includes bibliographical references and index.
ISBN 978-0-87417-676-6 (hardcover : alk. paper)
1. Civilian Conservation Corps (U.S.)—Nevada—History. 2. Young men—Employment—Nevada—History. I. Ford, Victoria, 1946– II. Title. III. Series.
S932.N4K65 2006
333.75'1609793—dc22 2006012658

The paper used in this book meets the requirements of American National Standard for Information Sciences—Permanence of Paper for Printed Library Materials, ANSI/NISO Z39.48-1992 (R2002). Binding materials were selected for strength and durability.

University of Nevada Press Paperback Edition, 2015
ISBN 978-0-87417-993-4

To all who served and those
who shared their memories

CONTENTS

ILLUSTRATIONS

Figures

Map

FOREWORD

The Civilian Conservation Corps (CCC) has generally been acknowledged by historians as one of the most popular and successful experimental programs of Franklin D. Roosevelt's New Deal. Established in 1933, it combined work relief and restoration and preservation of the natural environment. A review of major historical accounts published within the past decade on the New Deal, including biographies of Roosevelt and college history survey textbooks, indicates that interest by historians in the CCC has waned ever since Professor John A. Salmond published his monograph on the program in 1967. Conversely, those involved in historical preservation and oral history have simultaneously shown a strong interest in the CCC; many surviving camps and construction projects have fallen in various stages of deterioration, and time is short if they are to be preserved. Those survivors who participated in the program are now in their eighties or beyond, and oral historians have scrambled to obtain their personal stories. The authors have combined their training in historical preservation and oral history to produce a sparkling narrative that substantially advances our understanding of the era of the Great Depression in Nevada.

Initially, the CCC stimulated a great deal of controversy. Early decisions to utilize the army to manage the program and the reopening of several mothballed World War I military bases for orientation and physical-conditioning sessions for enrollees produced a flurry of concerns that FDR was scheming to use the CCC to create his own version of a militaristic Hitlerian youth organization. Those criticisms were soon silenced. The program demonstrated that it provided healthy and rewarding opportunities for young men who otherwise would have joined the ranks of the unemployed or, worse, become part of the horde of homeless wandering the land on foot and in railcars seeking adventure, work, and, in many instances, opportunities for mischief or criminal behavior. Critics came to view the CCC as a positive alternative to young men hitting the rods and roads.

Politicians of all persuasions learned from constituents that these young men received important medical attention (it was discovered during orientation sessions that more than one-third of the enlistees suffered from malnutrition or serious disease) and benefited from physical conditioning, nutritious food, and the opportunity to work in the outdoors. Federal and state officials were delighted with the resulting reforestation, flood control, fire control, and beautification projects. Many workers availed themselves of educational opportunities to complete their high school diplomas and enroll in technical-training courses during the evening hours.

Across the United States, CCC workers built campsites, hiking trails, picnic areas, wilderness shelters, and fire outlook towers; fought forest fires in the summer and floods in the spring; planted more than two billion trees in a stunning national reforestation effort; erected check dams to reduce soil erosion; and constructed fire lanes and wilderness roads to make the federal forests more accessible. Parents welcomed the twenty-five dollars sent home each month (the average worker was permitted to keep only five dollars of his monthly thirty-dollar stipend) and appreciated that their sons were off the streets and engaged in a wholesome endeavor. A few critics rightfully complained that the CCC offered no opportunities for women, and toward the end of the 1930s a few camps for women were opened and some 8,000 young ladies participated.

The CCC initially employed 250,000 young men after the enabling legislation sped through Congress during the first month of FDR's presidency (thus becoming one of a myriad of anti-Depression measures that became law during the New Deal's "First One Hundred Days"). Ultimately, nearly 3 million American men served in the CCC. By 1940, the CCC was generally considered to have become a permanent part of the American scene. That changed, of course, when young adults were needed for the epic struggles of World War II. By the summer of 1942, funding for the CCC had disappeared as FDR moved to put the nation on a wartime footing. "Dr. New Deal," he explained, had to be replaced by "Dr. Win-the-War." During the 1960s, fleeting images of the CCC resurfaced when President John F. Kennedy urged Congress to establish the popular Peace Corps, and President Lyndon B. Johnson incorporated the Job Corps and Volunteers in Service to America within his potpourri of Great Society programs.

Nevada, like other western states, was the recipient of New Deal funding far in excess of that received by more heavily populated midwestern and eastern states. It certainly got more than its equal share of CCC funding, and state leaders welcomed the CCC because there was much to be done and scant state funding with which to do it. As the pages that follow demonstrate, all of Nevada benefited from the many projects undertaken by the Civilian Conservation Corps. More than 7,000 Nevadans signed up, and they were joined by 24,000 men who came from elsewhere to work in the fifty-nine main CCC camps that were established across the state. Perhaps Nevadans never fully appreciated the contributions made by these workers until the program was abruptly terminated in 1942, leaving the state unprepared to deal with a long hot summer of devastating forest fires.

Persons interested in the history of Nevada are fortunate to have available one of the most comprehensive state studies of the Civilian Conservation Corps published to date. Renée Corona Kolvet and Victoria Ford provide a compelling narrative that emphasizes the human dimension of the program. Readers will learn how this special federal program restored and revitalized Nevada's forests and rangelands during the difficult time of the Great Depression. Not only do they provide a cogent history of the CCC in Nevada, but they also provide rich oral histories by former CCC workers and administrators. *The Civilian Conservation Corps in Nevada: From Boys to Men* is a most welcome new addition to the historical literature on Nevada.

Richard O. Davies
Foundation Professor of History
University of Nevada, Reno

PREFACE

As an archaeologist, Renée Corona Kolvet often came across the physical remnants of the Civilian Conservation Corps in remote corners of the state. She soon realized that archival information was hard to find and that there were very few local residents who remembered the Depression-era program. Although several federal agencies have prepared informative local or regional reports, there was no comprehensive history of the CCC in Nevada to be found. Thus, the idea for the Nevada Civilian Conservation Corps study was conceived and under way in 2000. Kolvet invited oral historian Victoria Ford to join the project so that oral history interviews could breathe life into the archival and archaeological record. Ford conducted the oral interviews between April and November 2000. Hence, this book represents the culmination of five years of research, enhanced by the personal recollections and experiences of CCC staff and enrollees once stationed in Nevada.

Kolvet embarked on an extensive data-gathering mission that took her to museums and record repositories across the country and required road trips around the state. Along the way, she met several longtime residents and local historians who helped her locate former camps or individuals who were familiar with the CCC program. To her surprise, she was able to physically locate or identify the former locations of the state's fifty-nine main camps. Today, scant traces of these facilities remain on Bureau of Land Management (BLM) land, private ranches, and mining properties or in state parks and national forests. Several sites were long ago obliterated by subdivisions, freeways, municipal parks, and roadside rest stops. As a result of this project, all camp locations were recorded and mapped for the first time, as detailed in the map shown in chapter 5.

Meanwhile, Ford set out to identify and locate CCC alumni who had spent time in Nevada. Though a few reside locally, the majority live out of state. The search for CCC alumni was gratifying. Harry D. Dallas, curator at the National Association of Civilian Conservation Corps Alumni (NACCCA) in St. Louis, Missouri, provided information on several alumni who were stationed in Nevada. Also, a news release was published in Nevada asking for volunteers who remembered Nevada's CCC camps or knew the whereabouts of CCC alumni. From those lists and volunteers, several chroniclers were located.

In reality, relatively few surviving members of Nevada's CCC are still around. Fortunately, those interviewed came from different backgrounds and held a variety of positions in the CCC—from supervisors to educators and laborers. But the men had much in common. They were determined to survive the hard times of the Great Depression. All saw the CCC as a means to help themselves and their families until the national economy improved.

Where possible, the oral history interviews were conducted in person, either in the chroniclers' homes, in offices, or in museums. Due to limited funding for travel, some distant interviews were conducted by telephone. A total of fifteen chroniclers contributed to this project, and the resulting eighteen audiotapes are archived at the University of Nevada Oral History Program (UNOHP) office on the University of Nevada, Reno campus.

Because oral histories are a primary source of information, for this project we chose to include complete quotes rather than paraphrase the CCC men's stories. Oral discourse in print lacks gestures, inflection, tone, and other nuances that make normal conversation lively and understandable. As much as possible, we have kept each person's original words. We have also used common oral history devices to represent the dynamic elements of spoken language: for example, "[laughter]" appears when the chronicler laughed in amusement. However, as with all oral histories, memory is imperfect, and the recollections may not be free of error.

We would like to thank the CCC alumni who contributed to this study: Claude Chadwell, Marshall Crawford, Calvin Cushing, Michael DeCarlo, W. D. Ferguson, Raymond Fry, Ralph Hash, Herman Haynes, Rex Hines, Harry Norman, Elmer Randall, Edmund Rosowski, Joseph Ruchty, and Vernard "Bud" Wilbur. At the time of the interviews, these individuals resided in the states of Nevada, New York, Florida, Missouri, Oregon, and California. We would also like to thank Dan Bennett of Midas, Nevada, for sharing his interview with Edna Timmons, conducted in October 2000.

ACKNOWLEDGMENTS

A comprehensive study of the Civilian Conservation Corps in Nevada could not have succeeded without the support and knowledge of many individuals. Our decision to conduct an archival and oral history study piqued the interest of many citizens, historians, and archaeologists. Our study officially got off the ground when Stephen Davis of the Nevada Humanities Committee agreed that there was a need for a book on this topic. A research grant from his organization helped defer our initial research and travel costs. Through the support of Dr. Pat Barker and a Challenged Cost Share grant from the Bureau of Land Management, we were able to document the location of Nevada's CCC camps and assist with the transcription costs of the oral histories. We especially thank cartographer Bob Estes for providing his technical expertise and drafting the CCC camp-location map. Shawna Green also helped scan photos. The University of Nevada, Reno's Oral History Program has agreed to publish a volume with the complete versions of the fifteen interviews conducted during this study. We thank Mary Larson of the University of Nevada Oral History Program for her generous support and encouragement throughout the process. We are particularly grateful to Dr. Richard O. Davies, history professor at the University of Nevada, Reno, for first reviewing the manuscript and writing the foreword.

Several museum and archival specialists assisted our information search. We appreciate the help of Harry D. Dallas, curator at the National Association of Civilian Conservation Corps Alumni in St. Louis, Missouri, and Dominic Santangelo of the California Conservation Corps Museum in San Luis Obispo. Archivists who offered assistance include the following National Archives and Records Administration (NARA) staff: Lisa Miller (Pacific Sierra Region), Eugene Morris (Archives II at College Park), and Raymond Teichman (Roosevelt Library). The knowledgeable Nevada Historical Society staff—Eric Moody, Marta Gonzales, and Lee Brumbaugh—repeatedly copied and photodocumented records and offered their knowledge. Kathy Totten at the University of Nevada, Reno's Special Collections Department was equally helpful. Curators around the state shared their local expertise. The list includes Bunny Corkhill of the Churchill County Museum, Virginia Tobiassen of the Old Logandale School, Georgeanna Main of the Mineral County Museum, Wally Cuchine of the Eureka County Museum, Dennis McBride of the Boulder City and Hoover Dam Museum, and the staffs of the Northeastern Nevada Museum and Virgin Valley Heritage Museum.

Many longtime Nevada residents shared their knowledge of former camp locations and CCC work projects in their areas: Bettie Parman, Lynn Gardella, and Sophie Shepherd of Cedarville, California; Russell Siders of Reno; Bob Maher of Lovelock; Bennie Hodges of the Pershing County Water Conservation District in Lovelock; Keith Gibson of McGill; Bob Dickenson of Ely; Dixie Whipple of Lund; Lee Ivey of Yerington; Joe Higbee, Cleo Connell, and Leo Stewart of Alamo; Emerson Leavitt and the late Bill Marshall of Logandale; and Brian Hafen, Gary Hafen, and Vincent Leavitt of Mesquite.

Several federal agency officials assisted in this study by providing records, articles, and photographs or by sharing their own CCC research. We thank the following Bureau of Land Management personnel: Margaret McGuckian (Winnemucca Field Office), Mark Henderson (Ely Field Office), and Robert (Randy) Mead (Carson City Field Office). Helpful employees of the U.S. Forest Service include Fred Frampton (Humboldt-Toiyabe National Forest), Kathleen Sprowl (Spring Mountain National Recreation Area), and Richa Wilson (Region 4 Office). Similarly, several employees of the U.S. Fish and Wildlife Service shared reports or scanned photographs: Lou Ann Speulda (Nevada State Office), Marti Smith (Ruby Lake National Wildlife Refuge), Bruce Zeller (Desert National Wildlife Refuge), and Virginia Parks (Region 1 headquarters). Thanks also to Steve Daron and Andi Kraft of the National Park Service, Lake Mead National Recreation Area for sharing archival photographs. Several Natural Resource Conservation Service employees offered their time and knowledge: Corey Lytle, Rick Orr, and Jarrod Edmunds. Others who enriched this study include Louie Delamonica from the Hawthorne Army Depot and Barbara Rohde and Steve Weaver from the Nevada State Parks Sysem.

In addition to our chroniclers (listed in the preface) we were pleased to meet and gain knowledge from the following CCC enrollees and staff or their families: enrollee Joseph Chmielewski (Camps Twin Bridges and Tuscarora); Camps Reno, Idlewild, and Minden commanding officer Lt. Col. (retired) John E. Wurst and his lovely wife, Jean; former California enrollee and CCC historian Harvey P. Herrington; and Mr. and Mrs. Robert G. Harmon, descendants of Camp Mill Creek superintendent the late William R. Black.

Finally, several people accompanied Renée into rural Nevada on data-gathering trips: they include Martin Einert, who traveled to Caliente to scan historic Soil Conservation Service photos; Ann and Ron Schreiber, who drove Renée through the Glendale Flood Control Works (and blew out two tires in the process); and finally, Renée's husband, Alan H. Simmons, who guided her through an unexpected snowstorm while looking for Camp Tuscarora and for his feedback on early drafts of the manuscript.

The Civilian Conservation Corps in Nevada

Introduction

Nevada is a state of many contradictions. The federal government owns nearly 90 percent of the land, which helps to keep its frontier spirit alive. Historically, its citizens have preferred to be independent of government regulation and unnecessary intrusions into their ways of life. The exception, however, was in the 1930s when a culmination of events and conditions forced even the proudest of citizens to reconsider this position.

By the early twentieth century, an increasing number of Nevadans were native born and intent on making a living off of the land. These descendants of the early pioneers were committed to staying and could not be dissuaded by hard times. Still, Nevada had the smallest population of any state in the Union. Outside of Reno, most towns were little more than frontier outposts or holdovers from mining's glory days. Major portions of the state lacked telephone service, electricity, and graded roads. Above all, Nevada was in dire need of economic diversity: mining remained the largest employer, with agriculture following as a close second. Although gaming was legalized in 1931, the industry did not become a significant source of state revenue until the onset of World War II.[1]

Environmentally, Nevada faced severe problems and lacked the infrastructure to control or contain the forces of nature and human abuse. Like much of the West, the arid state suffered from relentless droughts followed by devastating floods and insect infestations, all resulting in lost agricultural land. Prior to the enactment of federal range controls, cattle and sheep overgrazed the public domain. Stockmen watched helplessly as the natural forage dwindled away and the most desirable lands became unusable.

To make matters worse, the Great Depression occurred at the worst possible time for the Silver State. Low agricultural prices, catastrophic bank failures, mine closures, and a loss of jobs sealed Nevada's fate. Stockmen lacked the funds and workforce to address the environmental problems that threatened livelihoods. Then the price of minerals dropped so low that it was not worth the effort to mine them.

Newly elected president Franklin Delano Roosevelt and Nevada's national representatives recognized the conundrum faced by the federal agencies and Nevada residents. Congress quickly passed federal emergency measures to offer some relief. Pride and independence aside, the lingering Depression forced Nevadans to accept New Deal monies and the accompanying bureaucratic red tape.

As bad as it was (or seemed), Nevadans fared better than other states during the Depression years. The per capita federal expenditure was $1,130 in Nevada, the highest of all forty-eight states (1933–1939). Seventy-two percent of Nevada's federal spending went to three agencies: the Bureau of Reclamation (the Hoover Dam/Boulder Canyon Project), the Bureau of Public Roads, and the Civilian Conservation Corps.[2]

Scholars generally attribute the disproportionate share of New Deal funding to Nevada's political clout. President Roosevelt and Nevada's national representatives took care of each other. Senator Key Pittman was considered an asset to Nevada. As an unwavering ally of the president, Pittman served as president pro tempore of the U.S. Senate throughout the New Deal years. Both Senators Pittman and Patrick McCarran cast vital swing votes for New Deal programs. Not surprisingly, greater financial rewards went to states that solidly supported Roosevelt in 1932 and in his bid for reelection in 1936.[3] Thus, the president did not overlook Nevada's economic and ecological predicament, despite its low population.

Politics aside, western states with large land areas and small populations generally received larger-than-average federal allocations. In terms of CCC funding from 1933 through 1939, Nevada, Idaho, Wyoming, New Mexico, and Arizona received the highest per capita expenditures, while Ohio, Massachusetts, New York, and New Jersey were on the low end of the dole.[4]

A quick comparison of CCC camps in operation during the tenth CCC enrollment period (1937–1938) illustrates Nevada's favorable standing.[5] Based on the 1930 U.S. Census, Nevada (population 91,058) had sixteen camps, or one per 5,691 citizens; Arizona (population 435,573) had thirty-three camps, or one per 13,199 citizens; and New Mexico (population 423,317) had thirty-seven camps, or one per 11,441 citizens.

Early in his presidency, FDR set new priorities for social welfare and economic regulations. In Nevada, the most popular federal programs provided employment. Two early New Deal programs that provided jobs were the CCC (originally referred to as Emergency Conservation Work, or ECW) and, later, the Works Progress Administration (WPA). The WPA provided construction jobs on municipal and county buildings, schools, parks, and highways across the nation. Although 90 percent of the budget was earmarked for wages, WPA projects were generally regarded as wasteful and inefficient.[6] By contrast, the CCC was widely supported because it aided small, struggling communities and helped young men find a place in the nation's economic structure. Not surprisingly, the program was commonly referred to as the darling of the New Deal.

The CCC was the answer to the federal agencies' prayers. The program provided a free pool of labor that allowed them to implement a number of rehabilitation projects in record time. Within weeks of the CCC's creation, Nevada received four camps and dozens more were on the way. Between 1933 and 1942, more than 30,791 men were employed in CCC programs throughout the state. Since Nevada had few young men to spare, most enrollees came from eastern, midwestern, and, later, the southern states. The "boys," as they were called, received training while improving Nevada's forests, parks, wildlife habitats, irrigation systems, and rangelands.[7] The Division of Grazing (later the Grazing Service) administered the largest number of CCC projects because of the state's huge public domain.[8]

By 1934, Nevadans regained hope for range management with the passage of the Taylor Grazing Act. For the western states, this federal-private collaboration represented a monumental step toward gaining control over the open range. Despite the federal mandate, plans for massive range rehabilitation could not have been implemented without help from the CCC.

Statewide competition for CCC camps was rigorous and required political maneuvering. The program's economic benefits were far-reaching, and having a CCC camp in your community was a boon for local businesses. Camp personnel were advised to shop locally, and the young men also spent money in nearby towns. Following CCC rules, all but five dollars of junior enrollees' thirty-dollar monthly pay was sent to their families, which also benefited the participants' hometowns.

The CCC motto, "From boys to men in six months," accurately depicts the rapid transformation in the lives of these young men.[9] Their health and mental outlook improved as they learned skills, both on the job and through vocational courses taught in camp, which helped them find employment when the job market improved. As intended, the program built character, taught responsibility, and instilled hope for the future. A formal educational program was later added to the CCC program. Nationwide, more than forty thousand illiterate young men learned to read and write.[10] Like other Americans, Nevadans supported an ongoing, permanent CCC. However, World War II's huge demand for military troops and defense workers led to the program's demise.

While the events of seventy or more years ago place the CCC era in the not-too-distant past, few people can relate to the Great Depression or even understand why it occurred. Today, historians and economists continue to examine the factors that led up to the Great Depression and the political and economic motives behind the New Deal.

The intent of this book, however, is to raise awareness of this popular New Deal program, its ramifications to Nevada, and its benefits to the men who served. The melding of history and personal recollections helps capture the human side of this unparalleled effort to save a generation at risk. As members of the "Greatest Generation," the men's experiences often take us beyond Nevada and the Depression era.

Camp Tuscarora's education adviser and commanding officer posting vocational courses offered in camp, ca. 1939. Courtesy Special Collections, University of Nevada, Reno Library

The first four chapters of the book provide background and a context for the times. We describe the CCC program and its ramifications at the national, state, and local levels. The following seven chapters summarize the major CCC projects carried out under the direction of federal agencies in Nevada that supervised the undertakings. The final chapter is devoted to the CCC legacy, epitomized by the achievements and sacrifices of the enrollees whose strong backs and youthful optimism guided them through one of the most difficult times in recent U.S. history.

PART I

The Nation, Nevada, and the New Deal

1

A Nation Brought to Its Knees

> I was just out of high school in 1935, and most everybody was in the same boat that I was . . . farm boys. . . . My dad was hoboing in Canada. He saved every penny he made up there. . . . The idea when I originally enrolled was, the money I would make there [CCC], the folks were going to lay away for me, and I could go to college when I got out, which I wanted to do desperately. . . . Things were so bad that for a year and a half my parents, my brother, and my three sisters lived on my $25, so there was never a chance of me ever going to college.
>
> —Ralph Hash (Camp Newlands)

Like millions of young men, Ralph Hash graduated from high school only to find that there were no job opportunities or money available for a college education.[1] Worse yet, there were no job prospects on the horizon. American leaders feared for the future of this generation and with good reason—nearly fifteen million unemployed men were under the age of twenty-five. Of all Americans, young men were most affected by the Great Depression.

The Depression had entered its fourth year when Franklin Delano Roosevelt took office. Although he originally believed that relief was best handled by local and state agencies, the lingering economic stagnation forced him to reconsider his position. Big problems required big measures: the president decided that massive federal intervention was necessary to combat a crisis of such magnitude.[2] From that one starting point, his New Deal programs followed no single philosophy. He adopted some programs from the Hoover administration, and created others to alleviate emergencies or aid particularly depressed regions of the nation. A few New Deal programs such as social security have survived into the present, while others died along with the New Deal, as did the CCC.[3]

Most scholars will agree that New Deal programs offered hope and security to a nation gripped by fear and uncertainty. Public optimism soared when FDR pledged he would lead the country out of economic paralysis. His decisiveness and optimism alone inspired the American people.[4] The president's programs were structured to assist the economic fabric of the entire country and its people—from minorities, farmers, and recent immigrants to employers, bankers, and capitalists.

Roosevelt wasted no time in setting the wheels in motion, and the achievements of the Hundred Day Congress were impressive by any standard. All fifteen of the president's requests to Congress were signed into law by June 16, 1933. After tackling the banking crisis, cutting five hundred million dollars from the federal budget, and signing the Beer-Wine Revenue Act, he turned his attention to unemployment payments and other forms of relief. He created two new agencies: the Federal Emergency Relief Administration (FERA) and the Civilian Conservation Corps under the auspices of the Emergency Conservation Work agency. Although the statutory CCC was not created until June 28, 1937, the name Civilian Conservation Corps was used by the president and CCC officials with the creation of the ECW in March 1933. Their creation represents the first direct federal involvement in unemployment relief and welfare services in our nation's history.[5]

With Public Bill no. 5, the Seventy-third Congress created the ECW; the president signed it on March 31, 1933. Four years later, Congress passed and the president signed Public Bill no. 163, and the Seventy-fifth Congress reestablished the CCC for three more years beginning July 1, 1937. By then, seventeen- to nineteen-year-old enrollees represented 73 percent of the overall force. The youthful nature of the corps led to serious plans for a permanent CCC.[6] The CCC became one of the most popular New Deal innovations, designed to salvage two of the nation's most threatened assets—our young men and natural resources.[7] The CCC provided vocational training and full-time employment in a healthy outdoor environment. The program targeted unmarried men between the ages of eighteen and twenty-five (later expanded to include seventeen to twenty-eight year olds) living on public or private welfare and literally walking the streets hungry. Joseph Ruchty (of Camp Carson River) recalled the discouragement he felt while looking for work in Newark, New Jersey, in 1938. He had dropped out of junior high school to find a job and help his family:

> I struck out to go look for work with another fellow named Felix Lavertano. After looking . . . I said, "We're not going to find any work." We went down to the [Jersey] Shore and looked in places, and nobody was hiring . . . anybody. I used to stop

> at Edison's factory every morning until the guy, McCoy, knew me by sight. And when he'd see me coming in the door, he used to wave at me and say, "Hit the road." No jobs . . . When we came back home, then I went in the CC [*sic*] camps.[8]

The CCC helped solve another predicament—what to do with the "Bonus Army," the group of World War I veterans who averaged forty years of age in 1933. Many of the veterans suffered from poor physical and mental health or battle-fatigue syndrome.[9] Following the suggestion of veterans administrator Gen. Frank T. Hines, veterans were offered immediate employment with the CCC, which delayed wartime service bonuses that were demanded but not due until 1945.[10] Although some veterans scoffed at the one dollar–a-day compensation, thousands joined the CCC and soon found themselves conditioning and transporting new enrollees to camps around the country.

FDR's concept of shaping a sound environment while creating new jobs was nothing new. As governor of New York, he supported an amendment to the state constitution that culminated in the purchase and reforestation of one million acres of the state's abandoned farmlands.[11] On a national scale, Roosevelt was keenly aware of the environmental degradation that threatened the American countryside. Large expanses of public and private land suffered from massive neglect and shortsighted overuse. The Midwest and southeastern Atlantic seaboard were plagued by soil erosion, and Dust Bowl states lost precious topsoil due to poor farming practices. In the West, overgrazed rangelands and overcut forests coupled with droughts created conditions that were ripe for fire and erosion. By creating the CCC, the federal government provided environmental assistance to every state in the Union.

The sheer magnitude of mobilizing the CCC required synchronizing a huge workforce with a variety of government agendas. Executive Order 6101 required an advisory council to coordinate with the CCC director. The council consisted of one representative each appointed by the secretaries of war, agriculture, the interior, and labor. FDR appointed conservative labor leader Robert Fechner as the CCC's national director. Fechner answered directly to the president, and the advisory council communicated with the president through the director.

The president ordered that 250,000 unmarried men between the ages of eighteen and twenty-five be enrolled by July 15, 1933. Ultimately, that number increased to 274,375. Initially, the U.S. Army's role was to trans-

National CCC director Robert Fechner *(center)*, Irving Harris of the Bureau of Reclamation *(left)*, and Conrad Worth of the National Park Service *(right)* visit Hoover Dam in October 1937. Courtesy U.S. Park Service Collection, University of Nevada, Las Vegas Library port enrollees to the camps. It soon became apparent, however, that the army was best suited to running the camps. The army reluctantly agreed to the expanded role. The CCC also recruited 25,000 World War I veterans and another 25,000 local experienced men (known as LEMs) to train and supervise the inexperienced young men.

Enrollee Ralph Hash worked closely with military officers at Camp Newlands and recalls the unique relationship that the CCC had with the army: "We had regular army issue clothing, and army officers were our commanding officers, but it wasn't operated exactly like the military. They were still the bosses and we had to tow the line. Probably the major penalty they could have given us, if we were unruly and couldn't get along, they [would] just send us home."[12]

To meet the president's goal, 8,540 men had to be processed a day to occupy more than thirteen hundred "forest" camps nationwide.[13] By early May, there was doubt as to whether the goal was realistic. Labor Depart-

Enrollees were supplied with surplus uniforms and equipment, often World War I issue. This cartoon was drawn by enrollee Charles Maak (Boulder City Twin Camps) in 1936. Courtesy Boulder City Museum and Historical Society ment selection director W. Frank Persons discussed his concerns in a letter to Secretary of Labor Frances Perkins:

> I was startled this afternoon when told by Colonel Major that he estimates . . . only five hundred forest camps will be in operation by July 15th. . . . [At this rate] it will be nearly the first of October before 250,000 men are at work. . . . You will recognize that the organization we have created for the selection of men is a mighty engine of public opinion. It embraces the influential citizens in every township in all of the forty-eight states. . . . Naturally they are interested in these boys. . . . They are likely to manifest very actively any dissatisfaction . . . because the implied promises . . . (that is, a job in the near future) cannot be fulfilled.[14]

A new executive order was issued to streamline the mobilization process. Under the revised plan, project superintendents, technical advisers, and superintendents hired by federal agencies would maintain jurisdiction over the enrollees during work hours, while military veterans and reservists would be in charge of the men while in camp. The order also relaxed purchasing and bid standards, required the Department of Labor to complete selection of men by June 7, gave the army greater discretion in disciplinary matters over recruits, and approved 290 additional work projects by June 1.[15]

The War Department proudly reported to the president that it had successfully executed "the greatest peacetime demand ever made of the Army" on June 30, 1933. The army had organized 73 stations for use as reconditioning camps and received and performed physicals on more than 270,000 men. Within a few short months, the army transported 55,000 men (in 353 company units) from the East Coast and Midwest to 159 destinations in seven western states. By the July 15 deadline, 4,685 army officers—including 1,672 organized reserves and 510 navy and marine corps officers—were performing full-time duty.[16] Although a majority of enrollees served close to home, many were transported by train to destinations out West. Joseph Ruchty was one such person. Aspects of his selection and first trip out West were memorable, including the lack of sanitation.

Joseph Ruchty, Camp Carson River

Well, first you had to go and see . . . the overseer of the poor, Mary Nevills, and she wrote you up. . . . The next time they bring the allotment in, you go down to the Newark [New Jersey] Army. . . . It wasn't like you join the armed

A company of men en route to Camp Mill Creek disembark at Battle Mountain, ca. 1935. Photos by William R. Black from the collection of Mr. and Mrs. Robert G. Harmon

forces where you had to pledge allegiance to the flag and everything. We all wanted to be with the flag anyway. [From Camp Dix] they march you down to the railroad station, and you had your bags packed. And this is summertime, and you had your ODs—the winter clothes—on and you were perspiring. . . .

You had old Pullman sleepers, you know. Two guys would sleep on the bottom; one guy sleeps on top. Everybody tried to get to the top . . . [because] you're by yourself. Don't forget now, these are coal-burner trains. . . . The mess car is in the center of the train, two of them. And there's about four more cars on each side with recruits going into the camps. Now, they start with bringing the food to you. You got your old canteen cup, which was from World War I, and your mess kits were aluminum, World War I vintage, and you got that coffee. . . . Here comes the prunes. So by the time the next thing comes, the prunes [have] already been eaten. Then you get your bread, and then comes the apple butter. All it does is make the bread wet; apple butter was terrible. And then you got your eggs and potatoes. And then, that was it.

Now, you're coming back with your food and your mess kit, and all this—looks like pepper's getting over everything—it is cinders from the coal. So now you get back to your place, and you got quite a bit of cinders in your food.

Now, when you finish eating, here comes the . . . steaming hot water kettles. You dip your mess kits in there, right? Now, the grease is on the top, right? So when you pull it back up, the grease gets on it anyway. So you had to get into the washroom and do a little cleaning up with toilet paper. . . . But what the guys did, after each meal—they had the windows open because it was summertime—and they hit the side of your mess kit on the side of the train. Now when you got off that train, there was one streak of garbage all the way down.[17]

In a White House Press release dated July 3, 1933, an exuberant FDR announced that the goal of the American people had been met. He shared the following message to new enrollees in the ECW's periodical, *Happy Days:*

> It is my honest conviction that what you are doing in the way of constructive service will bring to you, personally and individually, returns, the value of which it is difficult to Estimate. . . . [Y]ou should emerge from this experience strong and rugged and ready for re-entrance into the ranks of industry, better equipped than ever. I want to . . . express to you my appreciation for the hearty cooperation which you have given this movement which is so vital a step in the nation's fight against the Depression and to wish you all a pleasant, wholesome and constructively helpful stay in the woods.[18]

The president was actively involved in the CCC's early progress. At first, with the help of his personal secretary, Louis Howe, FDR devoted considerable attention to every detail of the program, including the scope of the work and where the camps would be located. In time, however, the president's hectic schedule precluded his day-to-day involvement. He and First Lady Eleanor Roosevelt nonetheless remained personally interested in the CCC throughout its existence.

In nine years' time, the "Soil Soldiers" had completed an amazing amount of conservation work. New Deal supporters and public relations officials periodically released the CCC's long list of accomplishments and the latest statistics. By the end of the program, the CCC had completed 46,854 bridges, 3,116 fire lookout towers, 28 million rods of fencing, and 318,076 erosion check dams, in addition to thousands of campgrounds, range-control features, ditches, and canals.[19] Despite the CCC's overall success, the program was phased out by the summer of 1942. Most experts agree that the New Deal did little to end the Great Depression—instead, massive defense spending and World War II are attributed with the nation's economic recovery. At a press conference on December 28, 1943, President Roosevelt acknowledged the country's new priorities: "Dr. New Deal" saved banks, aided farmers, rescued the securities market, created jobs for the idle, built bridges and dams, and prescribed insurance for the elderly and unemployed. Now it was time for "Dr. Win-the-War" to take over.[20]

2

Nevada Fights Back

Nevada's population barely exceeded ninety thousand in 1930, making it the least-populated state in the Union.[1] Despite its sparse citizenry, the state received more than its proportional share of federal monies, due to three powerful Democrats in Washington, D.C.—Senators Patrick McCarran and Key Pittman and Congressman James Scrugham. At a Churchill County banquet, junior senator McCarran boasted: "We've brought into this state federal money in the amount of $1,500 for every man, woman, and child. . . . How much better Nevada has done than other states, some of which have received only $5 per capita."[2] The federal windfall was the result of several congressional acts directed toward remedying statewide problems. Laws were passed and federal monies were provided to stimulate the mining industry, promote tourism, and increase visitation to state and national parks, forests, and wildlife refuges.

Nevada's representatives not only were respected at home but also commanded respect from their colleagues in Washington, D.C. Nevada managed to hold its favored position despite known infighting among its three representatives and McCarran's well-known opposition to FDR's Judiciary Reorganization Act of 1937.[3] Fortunately for Nevada, senior senator Key Pittman was a faithful supporter of FDR and New Deal programs and held several influential positions. Pittman served as chairman of the prestigious Senate Foreign Relations Committee and became president pro tempore of the Senate in 1933. Considered a U.S. Senate insider, Pittman actively supported Nevada's mining industry.

In the 1932 election, Pat McCarran became Nevada's first native-born U.S. senator after beating Republican incumbent Tasker Oddie. The new senator wasted no time in building his power base in Nevada and Washington, D.C. He also landed key appointments to important committees, including Appropriations, Judiciary, Irrigation and Reclamation, and Public Lands and Surveys and gained strength in Nevada's Democratic organization.

Meanwhile, former governor and state engineer James Scrugham was elected to the U.S. Congress for the first time in 1932, where he served for ten years before running for the U.S. Senate. A strong advocate of recreation and tourism, Scrugham was instrumental in establishing several new parks around the state.

Initially, the Great Depression did not hit Nevada as hard as eastern metropolitan areas. By the winter of 1932–1933, however, an economic stalemate settled over the rural state. Marshall Crawford described the impact of the Depression on his hometown of Yerington, Nevada:

> I was just out of high school. I had been working on ranches and in grocery stores and wherever I could find work. I shined shoes sometimes. This was during pretty tough times in 1934. . . . There were seven of us in the family, and when

Congressman James Scrugham delivered the keynote speech at the dedication of Cathedral Gorge State Park in 1935. Courtesy Special Collections, University of Nevada, Reno Library

> my father died, I was fifteen years old. Why, then we had some troubled times. . . . My mother was no different from most of the other people around there—no way to make any money—so she washed and ironed clothes for people. Well, most families in Yerington were having a tough time.
>
> The economy of Mason Valley at that time was farming, so they raised potatoes, onions, alfalfa, and cattle. There were also a few merchants who were able to keep going. . . . The mines weren't going then, so it was really difficult. I was still living at home, except for those times when I was working on the ranches. Then, of course, I stayed on the ranches and had my meals on the ranches. . . . Everything that we could make, we all went together on.[4]

Not surprisingly, Las Vegas and Boulder City were little affected until 1935 when Hoover Dam was completed and several thousand dam workers were laid off.[5] Then, joblessness rose steadily and by June 1935, a total of 5,131 Nevadans were unemployed.[6] Company towns around the state were especially hurt. Production at Nevada Consolidated Copper Company in McGill dropped to 15 percent of capacity by the end of 1932. Most employees lost their jobs or were offered reduced hours. Company officials and the Red Cross tried to hold the community together by providing food for the needy and allowing employees with families to remain in company housing.[7]

Unemployed men from the Ely area sign up for jobs at Camp Lamoille in 1933. Courtesy Northeastern Nevada Museum

Nevada's main industries—mining and ranching—were soon crippled. Officials did what they could to shore up the industries that drove the state's economy. Senator Pittman, concerned over the drop in silver production, played a pivotal role in passing the 1934 Silver Purchase Act, which set the price the government had to pay for domestic silver.[8] Although the act aided silver producers, it left the copper industry—Nevada's largest mineral producer—in need of a priming. The National Industrial Recovery Act (NIRA), passed in 1933, offered some help. However, a copper code establishing the right of collective bargaining, minimum wage, maximum hours, and production limits barely got off the ground by the time NIRA was declared unconstitutional. As it turned out, revived unions and collective bargaining only briefly offered relief to Nevada's copper industry.[9]

Despite these measures, by 1938, the mining industry faltered again. The Public Works Administration and Works Progress Administration soon aided economic conditions, and mineral production began to resume its former role as Nevada's key industry. Nonetheless, most economists believe that wartime demands for copper in 1939 ultimately pulled Nevada's mining industry out of its long slump.[10]

One of the most acute financial tragedies, especially for the agricultural industry, was triggered by the closure of George Wingfield's banking chain on November 1, 1932. And panic spread like a wildfire. In a letter to his daughter, Senator McCarran wrote that the bank collapse "destroyed the financial and industrial life of the State of Nevada."[11] His prophesy nearly came true, but Nevada's congressional representatives and state officials managed to lessen some of the effects.

Stockmen were especially hurt since their profits from the sale of crops and livestock had been in a steady decline since 1928.[12] Economists blamed Wingfield's inability to diversify loans as the main reason for the bank failures. A longtime friend of the livestock industry, he did keep hundreds of sheep and cattle ranchers and farmers in business by extending or increasing their loans, despite insufficient collateral. When wool and livestock markets plummeted, the number of defaults and demands for renewals on existing loans soared. To his detriment, Wingfield continued to grant loans to beleaguered stockmen.

Struggling to stay solvent, Wingfield applied for federal loans from the Reconstruction Finance Corporation and other banks. His efforts proved futile. Once word of his financial problems circulated, anxious depositors panicked and withdrew their funds, creating a run on Wingfield's banks. Governor Fred Balzar intervened by declaring a bank holiday and tied up the remaining depositors' funds. But Wingfield assets were seriously over-encumbered, and the loans he was able to secure were not enough to stabilize the business. In the end, the Wingfield banking empire simply ran out of collateral, and his economic domination of the state came to an abrupt end.[13]

Following the banking collapse, scores of Nevada ranchers and farmers went bankrupt. Senator McCarran tried to help by rewriting the Frazier-Lemke Act. Previously declared unconstitutional, the act successfully passed in 1937, offering farmers a reprieve by allowing them to stay foreclosure proceedings.[14] At the same time, Pittman, McCarran, and Scrugham helped the remaining stockmen fend off foreclosures by reviving the Regional Agricultural Credit Corporation, which allowed stockmen to apply for funds to restock their ranches and pay off the scaled-down loans owed to Wingfield's defunct banks.

Meanwhile, other new problems demanded government action. Prior to the Depression, Nevada's small population had little need for a state welfare system. By 1933, a growing number of needy citizens forced the legislature to create the State Board of Charities and Public Welfare. Thereafter, the new board administered the incoming federal relief funds. Cecil Creel was appointed executive secretary of the board and director of Nevada's relief programs.[15] Creel also headed the short-lived Civilian Works Administration (CWA) in Nevada. (The CWA was subsumed by the Federal Emergency Relief Agency in 1934 and by the WPA in 1935.) Creel's appointment was also short-lived. By mid-1934, Senator Pittman and other prominent Democrats replaced the Republican with a political newcomer—Democrat Frank Upman Jr.[16]

Politics aside, the WPA successfully put thousands of Nevadans to work building roads, curbs, and gutters and constructing worthwhile municipal projects like swimming pools and golf courses. The WPA became the state's largest employer. Even artists, writers, and musicians were hired to work on art, theater, music, and writing projects nationwide.[17] In 1940, *The WPA Guide to 1930s Nevada* was published by the Nevada Writers' Project. New Deal programs successfully lowered the number of unemployed workers. An employment census dated November 20, 1937, listed Nevada's unemployed at 3,091, a reduction of more than 2,000 individuals since June 1935. According to the same census, the WPA, National Youth Administration, and CCC had provided employment to 1,385 men and 372 women in Nevada.[18]

Around the same time, and to the dismay of many residents, the state was forced to help a growing number of transients who escaped the depressed industrial and agricultural centers to the east. Thousands of migrant workers headed to southern Nevada in hopes of finding work at Hoover Dam. Oftentimes, transients en route to California became stranded in Nevada towns.

In Washington, D.C., FERA director Harry L. Hopkins was inundated with statistical data about the homeless. Confused by conflicting data, Hopkins hired investigator Lorena Hickok to assess the situation and report back on "the human aspects of the crisis." Basically, Hickok was charged with putting a face on the numbers.[19] The former newspaper reporter traveled across the nation and documented the economic status of small communities. In 1934, she visited Elko, Winnemucca, and Las Vegas. While in southern Nevada, Hickok learned that 7,000 people passed through the Las Vegas area each month. She was alarmed when she learned that unemployment was expected to rise dramatically following the completion of Hoover Dam. Hickok shared the grim situation in a letter to Winnemucca rancher Aubrey Williams: "The single men may drift away and may end up in transient camps. But what about those 1,500 families, with children? What about school? Where are they to go?"[20]

The transient problem in Nevada mirrored a nationwide dilemma, even more pronounced in East Coast cities. Camp Carson River enrollee Joseph Ruchty recalled a bleak scene at the Newark, New Jersey, train station after leaving Nevada in 1939. "I went back home. I went to Camp Dix . . . and they mustered you out from there. When we got to the Newark train station, a lot of hobos were out there. It's wintertime and they're cold. We had these old army coats, World War I coats, and a lot of us threw them to the guys."[21]

Nevada and the ten western states had little recourse but to accommodate the waves of men and families who passed through or settled in their state. Initially, government leaders wanted to restrict state relief efforts to Nevada residents. Once FERA grants were accepted, relief organizations and private charities extended relief to anyone in need, including those just passing through. In September 1933, Dr. George O. Smith of Reno was named Nevada director for transient relief.[22] He reported to Cecil Creel and later to Frank Upman Jr. Two relief depots, one in Reno and one in Las Vegas, were created, and other transient camps in Elko, Hawthorne, and Galena followed.[23]

Fortunately, CCC enrollees were better regarded than the migrant workers, despite their relief status. With few exceptions, the young men encountered little hostility or discrimination. After all, federal agencies and CCC officials attempted to educate the communities on the benefits of the program by inviting residents to the camp or speaking to service groups. Residents soon realized that the CCC program would benefit the communities by providing jobs for local men as well as the outsiders. Nevadans easily warmed up to midwestern and southern enrollees with farming backgrounds. These young men knew something about handling livestock and could drive and pitch hay. Missouri resident Ralph Hash was welcomed by Fallon residents when he arrived at Camp Newlands: "They were just beautiful people. They accepted us. You'd think a lot of them would be worried about their daughters, dumping a bunch of young men into a little town like that, but they weren't, because we had a good group of boys. We never had any trouble with any of our fellows. And the town, generally speaking, just accepted us with open arms."[24]

The CCC arrived in Fallon only to find rangelands and irrigation systems in serious need of a helping hand. Overgrazing, erosion, and drought challenged Nevada's livestock and farming industries and threatened their future. Acute drought conditions in 1932 and 1934 in Lander, Eureka, Esmeralda, Mineral, Nye, and White Pine Counties resulted in heavy losses to the agricultural industry. When the drought briefly subsided in 1936, the ensuing heavy precipitation and floods eroded rich bottomlands and ravaged stream banks. Water-storage facilities were ill-equipped to handle the vast amount of runoff, making flood control of Nevada's rivers even more crucial.

Senator McCarran was commended for tackling the problem. He was a strong supporter of flood control and promoted measures to harness and impound runoff waters that were normally unavailable to farmers during the irrigation season. The problems of the West were heard as far away as Washington, D.C.

Dignitaries including Nevada governor Richard Kirman Sr., Senator McCarran, and McCarran challenger Al Hilliard accompanied President Roosevelt on a train tour of the western states in July 1938. Fortunately, the exigency of the land seemingly overshadowed frictions between Senator McCarran and the president. These tensions stemmed from the senator's

President Franklin D. Roosevelt, Senator Patrick McCarran, and other dignitaries touring northern Nevada by rail in 1938. Courtesy Patrick McCarran Scrapbook, Nevada Historical Society

lack of support for certain New Deal programs and allegations of presidential court packing. The pensive president discussed Nevada issues with the delegation, including flood control for five rivers and the decline of the mining industry between short stops in Carlin, Sparks, and Reno. From the train's rear platform, President Roosevelt greeted large crowds that gathered along the way, reassuring them of his support: "I am glad to get back to Nevada. Nevada's population is altogether too small. I am water conscious and with the better use of water, Nevada's population would increase greatly. Nevada can support a much larger population. I have been studying the map, and the government is not forgetting the needs of Nevada."[25]

FDR and Nevada's representatives were well aware of the need to control water if agriculture was to prosper in the desert state. Problems with erosion weighed heavily on the minds of farmers and ranchers across Nevada, but particularly in the southeastern portion of the state. Based on need, several new CCC camps were established by the Soil Conservation Service (SCS). The CCC men were immediately put to work stabilizing riverbanks and building flood-control structures to slow bank cutting and soil loss along waterways, including the Muddy and Virgin Rivers and the Meadow Valley Wash.

CCC work on irrigation systems and flood control on private land remained a "gray area" throughout the nine-year program. At one point, CCC director Robert Fechner found it necessary to seek guidance from the president on the legality of this practice. In a letter to the president, Fechner mentioned a personal visit from Senator Pat McCarran and several gentlemen from his state on November 17, 1937. The Nevada contingent hand-delivered a petition from the privately owned Walker River Irrigation District requesting CCC help to construct new irrigation ditches. Fechner relied on the president to decide whether the private district should be granted a CCC camp. In turn, FDR expressed his disfavor with the practice, unless the situation was serious enough to force farmers onto relief roles. Fechner cited requests from other drainage-ditch associations:

> An identical condition exists in privately owned drainage ditch associations . . . that take water off of the land. [They] are wholly privately owned and any work we did on them would be solely for the benefit of private landowners. . . . On December 9th [1937] during a conference that you had with several members of Congress . . . including Honorable T. Alan Goldsborough of Maryland . . . you were not opposed to CCC work on this type of project. . . . We have at the present time approximately 42 CCC camps [nationwide] engaged wholly on drainage ditch projects. . . . In order that I may clearly understand your desires in the matter I will appreciate it if you will let me know whether or not we should continue these two types of work.[26]

Although FDR's directive is unknown, CCC projects on private land continued throughout the program. However, far more federal monies were invested in upgrading Bureau of Reclamation projects built soon after the turn of the century.

Even before the Depression hit, Nevada's irrigation systems, dams, and reservoirs were in need of serious maintenance and expansion. Irrigation systems built by the Reclamation Service (now the Bureau of Reclamation) were inadequate and showing their age. Canals were clogged with silt, and additional drains were needed to salvage waterlogged fields. Furthermore, rodents and weeds had all but destroyed canal and ditch banks. The Bureau of Reclamation acknowledged its responsibility to protect its earlier investments and assist struggling farmers. Thus, the CCC program provided a perfect mechanism for accomplishing both.

Nevada's rangelands and forests were also in need of attention. The Humboldt-Toiyabe National Forest (formerly Nevada National Forest) was covered with thick underbrush and a buildup of deadwood. Massive range and forest fires were feared.[27] To add to the dilemma, both range- and forestlands in northern Nevada were plagued by plant-eating Mormon crickets throughout most of the 1930s. Lander and Eureka Counties were considered disaster areas, even though Elko County was hit hardest.[28] Federal officials sought CCC help to build administrative facilities and lookouts, fight fires, reseed forests, and battle the scourge of insects "big enough to kill with clubs."[29]

Nevada's public rangelands also suffered severe soil depletion and vegetation damage following years of overuse and droughts. Overgrazing, lack of range management, and bitter competition between sheep men and cattlemen for limited forage had pushed the situation to a breaking point. Passage of the Taylor Grazing Act in 1934 established long-term goals to stabilize the western livestock industry by improving the condition of the range. Graziers wasted no time in preparing long lists of necessary improvements. One remedy was to open up additional rangelands in areas with high groundwater. This required the drilling of hundreds of new wells, many still in use today.

In addition to opening up new rangelands, improvements to existing ranges were necessary. The main undertakings included constructing new truck trails to connect winter and summer ranges and to provide access during range fires, erecting enclosures to prevent livestock damage near springs, and building earthen dams to impound winter runoff. To implement the provisions of the Taylor Grazing Act, the Government Land Office (soon the Division of Grazing and later the Grazing Service) and its first director, Farrington Carpenter, wisely sought CCC assistance.[30] By 1939, ranchers and state and federal officials had established several new grazing districts along with the rules and regulations to administer them.

Camp Hawthorne enrollee Bud Wilbur recalled working on roads and rehabilitating the range:

> After we passed our barracks inspection, we were turned over to the camp superintendent, who worked directly for the Division of Grazing. . . . And he had, what they called, Local Experienced Men (LEM): men that were qualified to teach us and lead us in the type of work that we were going to do.
>
> We graded roads. They had two graders in camp and a couple of DC-3 cater-

> pillar tractors, and they would assign you to a truck and to a foreman, with probably ten or fifteen men, or you might be assigned to stringing barbed wire or tightening barbed wire up—whatever the need was for the day.
>
> We dug out a big reservoir about a mile above the [Hawthorne] camp and firmed it all up with rocks and so forth, and then it was filled so that the stockmen could use it for drinking water for cattle—a reservoir for water. It might have been . . . a hundred yards square. . . .
>
> Also, quite often we would go out on a range and sort of attempt to grade it out and level it out, take away unwanted type cactus that was there, that the cattle used to feed on, which was not good for them. . . . We covered a lot of area around Hawthorne, probably anywhere out to thirty or forty miles out into the desert.[31]

The CCC came to the aid of other federal and state agencies, such as national and state parks and the U.S. Fish and Wildlife Service (FWS). Officials were confident that improved road systems and better access to remote regions of interest would stimulate tourism and attract new residents. Local officials marketed Nevada's unique qualities and frontier attitudes. The City of Reno and the local Lions Club circulated brochures that welcomed visitors, highlighted Reno's scenic attractions, and listed the mileage to suggested destinations. Also promoted were Nevada's less stringent driving codes and the fact that out-of-state motorists were exempt from arrest for ordinary traffic violations.[32]

The Nevada legislature was also instrumental in obtaining land for parks. With help from the Daughters of the American Revolution (DAR), the restoration of Fort Churchill became a reality. Creating new parks meant building campgrounds, hiking trails, and access roads and parking lots—projects suited to the CCC. Congressman Scrugham aggressively fought for CCC assistance in developing Nevada's parks.[33] Southern Nevada especially benefited, and the first state parks were built at Valley of Fire near Las Vegas in 1934 and Cathedral Gorge near Caliente in 1935.

Federal and Nevada officials acknowledged the need to build refuges for the protection of migratory waterfowl and local wildlife. The WPA and CCC helped construct new facilities and access roads at Charles Sheldon National Wildlife Refuge and Ruby Lake National Wildlife Refuge, both in northern Nevada, and the Desert National Wildlife Refuge in southern Nevada. (The federal CCC programs and respective projects in Nevada are discussed in part 2 of this book.)

Nevada's elected officials, businessmen, and citizens continued to seek ways to combat the economic slump. Not surprisingly, gambling was legalized in 1931 to attract more visitors to the Silver State and to generate taxable revenue. Nevada's fast-track divorces, with only a six-week residency requirement, also enticed divorce seekers from the other forty-seven states.

The state's cultural and historical heritage had the potential to attract new visitors, but most attractions were off the beaten path. Developing parks and recreation areas and better access were pet projects of Congressman Scrugham. He also was intensely interested in Nevada's prehistory. Southern Nevada sites, such as the Lost City, were salvaged before being inundated by Lake Mead, forming behind Hoover Dam. The CCC was assigned to several archaeological projects and built the Lost City Museum facility for artifact storage and public education.

Basically, the CCC significantly helped the economy and infrastructure around the state. CCC works can still be observed in national and state parks and wildlife habitats and in the form of improved roads, wells, dams, irrigation ditches, and water troughs scattered across rangelands.

3

The CCC Program in Nevada

Nevada seemed like a foreign country to many of the young men from the urban East Coast, wooded South, and midwestern heartland. Some enrollees never adjusted to the treeless landscape with saline playas, blustery winds, and so few people. The paramilitary lifestyle also caused uneasiness in some young men. Despite frequent bouts of homesickness, the majority completed at least one six-month commitment. More adventurous enrollees enjoyed Nevada's desert and small-town appeal; some reenrolled for up to three six-month hitches. In fact, many men found permanent work, married, and never left Nevada. One such enrollee was midwesterner Ralph Hash, who vividly recalled his angst while waiting for the train to Fallon:

> I didn't know anything about Nevada. . . . It was just a name to me. When I first saw Nevada, well, I tell you my heart almost sank. We came by rail. . . . The main line of the Southern Pacific comes through Hazen, Nevada, but there was a little splinter line off of Hazen that ran to Fallon, because they had a little "tooterville trotter" that ran from Reno to Fallon. Well, they pulled us on the siding out there at Hazen, and there we sat, in the middle of the afternoon. And we looked out the windows and saw nothing but old white alkali flats and the scrubby brush here and there.
>
> I go, "Oh [with sigh]! Are we going to be stationed here? What in the world . . . ?" Well, everybody was about to panic. We sat there for about two hours before they got an engine to haul us all into Fallon. Once we got there, it was fine. That's a beautiful little town. I didn't know anything but little towns anyway. Beautiful. Yes, I was really tickled. It had trees and lawns.[1]

Enrollees' attitudes and experiences were often expressed in poems that served as creative outlets for the young men. The following is an excerpt from a camp newspaper, the *Camp Newlands Courier:*

> Out of the camp and into the fields,
> Every dreary morn,

I cuss the lieutenants and the C.O. too,
That I was ever born,

Work all day in the blistering desert,
Hot as scriptural Hell,
Cussing the boss and the officers too,
Hating their silly yell.

The insects, snakes, and lizards,
Belong in the desert, not me,
The pick and shovel should be in camp,
Or back in the factory.

Building culverts and cleaning canals,
And always digging trenches,
Building levees and fighting fires,
And once in awhile, some fences.

Then back to the bunk each evening,
Dirty, hot, and raw,
Sometime I think I'll up and say,
"This life gets in my craw."

Bemused CCC recruits linger for several hours at Hazen while awaiting a train into Fallon, 1938. Courtesy Churchill County Museum and Archives

I grip and fume and fuss and fret,
Till hatred turns to gall,
And threaten murder, mayhem, death,
To all within my call.

And then we have some baseball games,
Some shows or a fight or two,
A drink with a pal and a date with a gal,
And my cussin' will kinda slow.

Next thing I know the officer smiles,
And hands my pay to me,
Then I smile and sing and yell aloud,
"Three cheers for the CCC."[2]

State Quotas

Nevada's representatives frequently touted the state's good fortune in obtaining substantial federal relief funds. As stated in the introduction, Nevada reaped proportionately higher benefits from the national CCC program and was awarded more camps and enrollees per capita than other states. Its sizable federal land holdings, passage of the Taylor Grazing Act, and active representation in Washington, D.C., tipped the balance in Nevada's favor.

The number of camps assigned to Nevada fluctuated by agency and time periods. During the CCC program's nine-year existence, fifty-nine main camps operated around the state, often simultaneously.[3] Eighty-three different companies organized in the East, the Midwest, or the South were stationed in Nevada. CCC companies commonly transferred from project to project and state to state once a mission was accomplished. The earliest camps were assigned to the Forest Service, national and state parks, the military reservation (that is, Hawthorne Naval Depot), and Soil Conservation Service projects in southern Nevada; however, toward the end of the CCC program, Grazing Division projects on public domain dominated. Only ten Nevada camps remained in operation at the close of the program in 1942. Broken down by supervisory agency, the Nevada CCC camps consisted of 26 under the Division of Grazing/Grazing Service (including Camp Idlewild, a special detachment of Camp Minden); 7 under the U.S. Forest Service; 6 under the Soil Conservation Service and/or private land erosion (performing soil-erosion work on private land); 6 working in state and national parks; 5 under the Bureau of Reclamation; 4 under the Bureau of Fisheries/Biological Survey/Fish and Wildlife Service; 3 working for private entities; and 2 working for military agencies.

The number of enrollees who served in the CCC was influenced by national quotas, state quotas, government-agency program requests, and the number of camps in operation at a given time. The size of the Nevada CCC program fluctuated over time. For example, between the end of 1935 to November 1936, the number of CCC men working in Nevada increased from 2,626 to 3,000. Of this number, 421 were nonenrolled personnel (LEMs or foremen), 59 were Native Americans, and 13 were nonenrolled personnel with the CCC Indian Division.[4]

Nevada's meager population meant it had the smallest quota in the country. Veterans' quotas were even smaller since the national quota was not to exceed 27,200 at any one time. The national CCC director set the veterans' quota for districts in the Ninth Corps area at 2,000.[5] Broken down by territories, the quotas were as follows:

Northern California (headquarters San Francisco)	535
Southern California (headquarters Los Angeles)	627
Idaho (headquarters Boise)	90
Montana (headquarters Fort Harrison)	110
Oregon (headquarters Portland)	194
Utah (headquarters Salt Lake City)	104
Washington (headquarters Seattle)	320
Nevada (headquarters Reno)	20

The national CCC director estimated that during the first five years of the program (from April 1933 to June 30, 1938), a total of 5,519 Nevada men were given employment in CCC projects. Of these, 3,762 were enrollees (juniors, veterans, and Indians) and 1,757 were nonenrolled personnel (reserve officers and work supervisors). According to Camp Paradise foreman Wilbur Timmons, there were few prospective enrollees available in Nevada: "Of course, a lot of the boys who had no work were from the East. You see, we didn't have that many [men] in Nevada. They couldn't have gotten local men. The farm work took care of a lot of young fellows."[6]

Midway through the CCC program, the majority of Nevada camps were administered by the Department of Grazing. To illustrate, the twenty-four Nevada camps in operation on October 20, 1938, were under the direction of the following federal agencies: U.S. Forest Service (National Forest), one; Bureau of Reclamation, two; private entity (private forest), one; Division of Grazing, seventeen; Soil Conservation Service, one; and National and State Park Services, two.[7]

Continued implementation of the Taylor Grazing Act, with its emphasis on rangeland rehabilitation, contributed to the increase in Division of Grazing camps in 1938. In fact, the number of enrollees in Nevada actually grew at a time when national enrollment was declining. To illustrate, national CCC enrollment decreased from 300,000 to 250,000 as of July 1, 1938. In Nevada, however, the upward trend continued. By May 31, 1939, Nevada enrollees reached an all-time high of 4,449, consisting of 4,341 juniors, 105 project assistants, and 3 veterans.[8]

By 1938 the CCC program began to train the men in skills that would contribute to the nation's defense. Despite Nevada's ambitious conservation goals, rumors of a global war and a gradual upswing in the economy led to a reduction in CCC work programs. Statistics reflect a scaled-back CCC program in July 1941 when statewide strength fell to 2,706 men—roughly half of the workforce reported two years earlier. The CCC continued to release a sizable number of enrollees into the private sector until the number of camps in Nevada diminished to 16 (of 1,096 nationwide) in September 1941. By the close of the program in July 1942, a total of 7,079 Nevada men had been employed by the CCC—3,781 junior enrollees and veterans, 970 Native Americans (working on reservations), and 2,328 nonenrolled personnel. Collectively, Nevadans (enrollees, veterans, Native Americans, and nonenrolled personnel) represented slightly less than one-fourth of the 30,791 men who were employed in Nevada's CCC program.[9]

Organization and Selection

Upon learning of its new role, the U.S. Army described itself as the "surprised and bewildered foster parent of a quarter of a million young men."[10] Still, the army was best suited to managing a large all-male workforce. Nevada was one of seven western states assigned to the army's Ninth Corps Area with its main headquarters in San Francisco, California. As for direct administration, Nevada was assigned to a three-way split: the Sacramento District headquarters provided administrative and logistical support for camps in northern and central Nevada and northern California, the eastern portion of the state was administered by the Fort Douglas (Utah) District headquarters, and the southern portion of the state (south of Hawthorne) was administered by the Los Angeles District headquarters.

The Department of Labor (DOL) established each state's quota based on its population. The DOL communicated the Nevada quotas directly to the head of CCC selection, initially Cecil Creel. Requisitions for the quotas to be filled were sent quarterly to each state selection agency. Enrollment quotas were evaluated every three months—in January, April, July, and October. The state directors then divided the requisition by the respective number of local government relief units.[11] In Nevada, county relief agents were usually responsible for recruiting a specified number of qualified individuals. Smaller communities did not always fill their quotas.

Although national standards of eligibility guided the selection process, the criterion for establishing public relief rolls was different in each state. This prompted the national DOL director to send questionnaires to each state for clarification. In Nevada, state selection director Gilbert Ross responded that all CCC applicants or their families must be certified to the WPA or receive relief from the State Board of Charities and Public Welfare, or their dependents must be receiving local funds from programs such as Old Age Assistance or Mothers' Pensions.[12]

Details of the selection process were covered by the *Reno Evening Gazette.*[13] A quota of 96 Nevada men was established for six Bureau of Reclamation camps in Reno, Tahoe City, Topaz Lake, Lovelock, and Fallon. Applications were received at the new post office building in Reno. Depending on qualifications, applicants would receive from thirty to forty-five dollars per month and all subsistence. Although men from nearby communities were sought for each camp, Reno men would oftentimes fill openings in the absence of local applicants.

Clarence Thornton, an employee at the University of Nevada, Reno's Agriculture Extension Service, coordinated between Nevada's rural relief offices and the state CCC selection office while Creel was director. Thornton's job was to screen and register the recruits. Once accepted, army and navy doctors from Sacramento conducted the physical examinations on new enrollees. An enrollee had to be in good overall condition to join. Immediate dental needs were usually handled locally. According to Thornton, boys with bad teeth were sent to Reno dentist Dr. Rhodes, who charged five dollars to pull a tooth. In the interest of time, many young men were hastily processed, making fillings or other tooth repairs impractical. Thornton recalled, "One afternoon, about three o'clock, [Dr. Rhodes] called up and told us not to send any more boys down, that his arm was sore from pullin' teeth."[14]

Once inducted, enrollees in some rural camps had to travel for dental care. Camp Ruby Lake enrollee Herman Haynes recalled having a tooth extracted for a mere two dollars during a recreational trip to Elko.[15]

Recruitment in southern Nevada was coordinated through county extension agent J. H. Wittwer's office.[16] To fill 200 openings at the new Charleston Mountain camp, Clark County was allotted 179 out of a statewide quota of 750 Nevada men, second only to White Pine County. Enrollees were sent to Las Vegas doctor T. P. Ragsdale for their physicals.[17] In rural areas, army doctors often traveled between camps to administer immunizations and conduct physical examinations. Enrollee Marshall Crawford recalled the part-time medical and dental care at Camp Hawthorne:

> That's where I broke my tooth. . . . I was working on the roof, and I was driving nails down through the tarpaper. . . . I had nails in my mouth; and somehow or other, I got one in between my teeth, and I slipped on that roof and I made a grab . . . trying to keep from falling off the roof. When I did, I must have clamped down, so I lost the tooth. They had a dentist there, and he pulled out what was left of the tooth. . . . I think the doctor and dentist just visited: they didn't stay full-time.[18]

Medical care and staffing levels differed between camps. At Camp Newlands in Fallon, Ralph Hash recalled that full-time medical care was available: "We had a full-time camp doctor. He was part of the company. He had a regular sick bay. . . . It might have been where the recreation room barracks was—part of that. He had his own office and a bed or two where he could take care of kids. We never had any serious sicknesses while we were there."[19]

Once in the CCC, physical fitness was an important part of the program. Most of the men were in prime condition as a result of regular wholesome meals, morning calisthenics, and physical labor during work hours.

Nevada Enrollee Profiles

State selection agencies periodically prepared statistical reports for the DOL. The director of camp education filed additional data with the national CCC director. From the available reports, some rough statistics and comparisons can be made. The limited data provide insights into the vital statistics of Nevada residents in the CCC. For comparative purposes, officials often added national program data. Unfortunately, national and Nevada reports with similar dates were seldom available. Nonetheless, there is little evidence of ethnic diversity in Nevada's CCC program. Furthermore, black enrollees played a relatively minor role in the Ninth Corps area in contrast to corps areas in the East and South. A review of available DOL "Summaries of Statistical Data" reports showed no evidence of black enrollees in Nevada. Similarly, black enrollees were negligible in the neighboring state of Utah. A DOL "Summary of Statistical Data" prepared on January 6, 1939, reflects an enrollment strength of 1,237 junior enrollees. Of the general population, 99.8 percent were listed as "white" and 0.2 percent were "colored."[20] The absence of blacks was obviously intentional. CCC officials went to great lengths to avoid problems with rural communities.

Whereas approximately 10 percent of the national CCC workforce was black, a small number of black enrollees were stationed at designated Ninth Corps–area camps in Idaho and Wyoming. By August 1935, however, all black enrollees in the Ninth Corps area were segregated and transferred to five all-black camps in California, despite a nondiscrimination policy.[21] Another twenty years would pass before the Civil Rights Act put an end to segregated groups in government programs.

Age Distribution and Physical Characteristics

Very few of the seventeen- and eighteen-year-old recruits had prior work experience, so a major goal of the CCC was to teach them job skills. Older men with families and work experience usually landed what few jobs were available, leaving few opportunities for the up-and-comers. Thus, the CCC program appealed to the very youngest men. According to two 1935 DOL surveys, of the 289,705 men enrolled during the summer and fall of 1935, more than 67 percent were under twenty-one years of age. When the eligibility age was lowered to seventeen in October 1935, the numbers of seventeen- and eighteen-year-old junior enrollees were nearly equal. Collectively, they composed almost half of the total national enrollment that month.[22]

Age distribution among Nevada residents in the CCC appeared in line with the national statistics, based on a DOL report for June–August 1935 enrollment. Of 68 Nevadans enrolled during this period, 28 (41 percent) were eighteen years of age, and 11 (16 percent) were nineteen years old. Thus, 57 percent of Nevada's CCC boys were under twenty, and the remaining 29 (or 43 percent) were over twenty years of age.[23]

A 1940 DOL report lists the height and weight of 42 Nevada juniors accepted for enrollment. According to this report, the majority of men stood between five feet six inches and five feet eight inches tall and weighed between 137 and 151 pounds. The weights listed were most likely greater than the preenrollment weights. According to the national CCC director, Robert Fechner, "On an average, these men gained about ten pounds . . . during their first three to six months of service."[24]

Education and Urban/Rural Classification

National CCC statistical reports show that 63 percent of enrollees selected during the year ending June 1937 never attended high school. The percentage appears to have improved during the last four years of the program. Two 1938 reports for Nevada enrollees reflected a slightly higher level of education. An enrollment report for January 1940 indicated that 40 percent (17 of 42 enrolled) never attended high school. Nine months later, the same report showed a reduction to 32 percent (9 of 28 enrolled).[25] Based on limited data, we can surmise only that Nevada enrollees were staying in school longer due to the recovering economy.

Of the fourteen CCC alumni interviewed for this study, three had not completed high school when they enrolled: Calvin Cushing had three years of high school, Rex Hines was only fifteen or sixteen years old when he enrolled, and Joseph Ruchty had a junior high education. Bud Wilbur actually earned his high school diploma while in the CCC.

A majority of Nevada enrollees came from urban as opposed to rural areas, according to two reports from the state CCC director's office. This is not surprising, given the shortage of men available to work in agriculture. Of the 26 Nevadans enrolled as of July 1937, 66 percent were from urban areas and 34 percent were from rural districts—a ratio of nearly two to one. These findings roughly coincide with Nevada's population distribution, with 62.2 percent of Nevadans living in rural areas as of 1930. A similar report for the January 1941 enrollment revealed that 69.5 percent of the 23 Nevada junior enrollees were from urban areas, whereas only 30.5 percent were from rural communities.[26] Interestingly, the rural enrollees were from small towns, and none came from farms or ranches.

4

Outsiders and Small-Town Folk

Commerce

The fortunate communities that were granted CCC camps welcomed the federal funds that trickled into their economies. However, competition to obtain a new camp was stiff and required considerable lobbying from both the community and its national representatives. An editorial in the *Mineral County Independent* of Hawthorne summarized how the hard work of local officials paid off:

> It is difficult at this time to estimate the full value the camp will prove to the Hawthorne district. Of primary interest is the amount of money to be directed into channels of trade. . . . Greater will be the improvements to be made . . . at the naval depot. Yet the experience of working to have the camp established here has not been lacking in beneficial teaching. It has taught that in order to obtain things for the county and community, the people must work together and they must work. . . . We commend Judge Ferrel for his efforts. . . . Everyone will agree that Captain H. S. Babbitt more than anyone, played a leading role in the campaign to get the camp. . . . [W]e feel the utmost credit is due District Attorney Fred L. Wood, who fostered the movement.[1]

Communities with a CCC presence reaped both direct and indirect benefits. Local men were hired as foremen (LEMs) and earned a much-needed paycheck. Some continued to keep their own businesses going while waiting for an upswing in the economy. Enrollee Calvin Cushing of Camp Hubbard Ranch described the life of foreman Joe Mellan:

> Well, he was one of our camp field managers, and he lived in Tonopah, Nevada. On weekends he would go home and work on a gold mine . . . between Tonopah and Wells, that's quite a distance. . . . They'd . . . leave on a Friday night after work and then be in camp for Monday morning's work . . . because most of them had families at that time. He was a LEM, local experienced man. I'm sure the superin-

> tendent of camp brought in men that could do different work in the field, but seemed like they were all mostly in their forties.[2]

In addition to providing jobs for Nevadans, the CCC purchased supplies from local merchants.[3] Construction materials were always obtained locally, but food supplies were another matter. Only after a series of complaints were perishables added to the list of local purchases. Outraged merchants and the Chamber of Commerce complained to Senators McCarran and Pittman after a truckload of food supplies en route to Camp Fort Churchill was spotted driving through Reno. The senators complained to the quartermaster's office in Sacramento and Ninth Corps Area headquarters in San Francisco. The issue was quickly resolved.[4]

Competitive bids were sought locally for construction materials to build the camps. A newspaper editorial wisely reported that the biggest order was for supplies to build the winter camp at Hawthorne. Learning from past mistakes, the army routinely itemized and made public the dollars spent in Nevada towns. The expenditures were considerable. According to a Reno newspaper, the Hawthorne and Fort Churchill camps spent $48,588 in local communities during the first year and a half of the CCC program, and even more business was expected. With plans to build six new camps within a one hundred–mile radius of Reno, the army estimated that close to $300,000 a year would be expended in the region.[5]

In addition to funds spent by the CCC, enrollees patronized local theaters, dance halls, cafés, skating rinks, and grocery stores. Men stationed near towns had more opportunities to spend their earnings than those living in rural camps. In fact, the commanding officer at Camp Reno complained that his men purchased personal items, including candy, cigarettes, and stationery supplies, in town as opposed to the camp canteen.[6]

A few enrollees in each camp earned more than thirty dollars per month, depending on their work assignment. To Calvin Cushing the pay raise he received to help supervise the camp was most welcome:

> We went to town I'm sure, on the weekends or on Saturday anyway. But on five dollars a month you didn't go too many places at that time. Twenty-five dollars went home, and we got five dollars. . . . And then as you went up the ladder, the most you could make was twenty dollars a month more, which you got and still twenty-five went home. I have no idea how I got the rank of first sergeant. The first sergeant at that time went home and there was an opening. . . . They gave me a fifteen-dollar increase in my pay, which was all right.[7]

An added benefit of CCC wages was the financial boost to the enrollees' home states. According to the War Department, enrollees in Nevada camps sent an estimated $844,000 to their families between April 1933 and November 30, 1935.[8]

Personal Impressions

The influx of enrollees from East Coast cities intimidated some local residents, but only until they got to know them. New Yorker Bud Wilbur of Camp Hawthorne recalled, "At first the townspeople treated us as though they had been invaded by New York gangsters. This attitude proved to be short-lived, however, and locals developed a community association that urged CCC participation in community events."[9]

Indeed, the community of Hawthorne went the extra mile to encourage CCC participation in sports competitions, amateur theater, and even mock trials. Surrounding communities such as Fallon also learned that the CCC was a good thing. Although the men were initially accepted with "some coolness," Fallon residents soon recognized the value of the program once they became aware of the improvements being made to their irrigation systems.[10] Overall, the men created few problems for the communities. At a Fallon Rotary Club Flag Day presentation, district court judge Clark Guild praised the CCC's clean record: "Very few boys of the CCC camps get into real trouble . . . no greater than any other group of boys. . . . I have never heard of one word of condemnation against this great movement of the CCC."[11]

But in some communities, attitudes toward enrollees were mixed. Oral interviews and correspondence from former camp superintendents, commanding officers, foremen, enrollees, and Nevadans offer a broad range of views toward the outsiders. A few reflect underlying biases against "city boys." For example, foreman Andy Jackson from Camp Gerlach had strong opinions about some of the men: "The CCC did a lot of good. Most of the kids were from the city and from the poorer classes. . . . [T]hey learned how to work. There were 275 . . . and there were 25 of us local guys, and they'd get out in the sun and they'd faint. They'd cut their finger and get blood poisoning."[12]

Wilbur Timmons, a foreman at the forest service's Camp Paradise, worked closely with the young enrollees. He recognized their "culture shock" and realized that many of the men lacked even the most basic skills:

> We had boys right from the Bronx and some of them never drove a truck, never drove a car, in their lives . . . and we had to have an average of twelve to fifteen drivers [that] we had to get out of that [group] some way or another . . . and that was my job. . . . But we had an exceptional crew from Kansas. Those boys were mostly farm boys who got knocked out of work from that sandstorm that covered up all their country. . . . We had some very good help from there. . . . The eastern boys, we had quite a time with them, and yet we had a few good ones. . . . New York boys weren't used to the environment here. . . . The other boys from the South and the Midwest were more oriented to the environment.[13]

Lewis B. Jeannay, superintendent at Camps Sunnyside, Cherry Creek, and Golconda, also noticed differences between enrollees from around the country. Jeannay referred to men from Illinois, Kentucky, Tennessee, and Georgia as "good boys" and those from Brooklyn and New Jersey as "tough bastards." Some of the youths had a history of fighting and altercations with the law. Jeannay specifically remembered the "Mohicans" who arrived in Ely with Mohawk-style haircuts. The group created quite a stir and repeatedly clashed with the local law enforcement.[14]

Jeannay's recollections are supported by enrollee Rex Hines from Camp Indian Springs, west of Ely. The Kentuckian shared his impressions of the "northerners" in his camp:

> The CCC boys had a tough reputation for being rowdy. I know they did, just from talking to them in camp and hearing what happened when they were in town. . . . They had a reputation for being fighters, because so many of these guys were from up north. . . . Most of them were sort of hard to get along with. There weren't too many of us . . . southern boys . . . that I remember. The southern boys were easier to get along with.[15]

The army occasionally had to take extra steps to keep order. Retired lieutenant colonel John E. Wurst, commanding officer at Camps Reno, Idlewild, and Minden, was sent from New York to handle growing dissent at Reno-area camps. Despite the easterners' tough reputations, Wurst was sympathetic to the loneliness that they felt:

> All members of my camps came from New York and New Jersey. Most of the men had never been away from home, and it was tough for some of them. I tried my best to help them get acclimated to CCC life. . . . Some of them cried themselves to sleep. . . . I was originally assigned to Camp Reno. They were having trouble and I was sent there to straighten things out. Being a "New Yorker" I was more accustomed to New Yorkers. We are a special breed of cats. The CCC and

> Reno, Nevada, was the biggest and best thing that ever happened to me. There, I met my wonderful wife. . . . She worked for Gray Reid and Wright. . . . We have been happily married since 1938.[16]

Loneliness was a recurrent theme. William "W. D." Ferguson, from Oakland, California, clearly remembered the isolation of living at Camp Westgate in 1939:

> I was eighteen. Just got out of high school. . . . Let me tell you the worst part. It was my loneliness, homesickness. First time I had ever been away from home. . . . I used to go out to the desert at nighttime, be by myself, and cry a little bit. . . . I was close to my mother, and I got letters. I probably noticed others who were homesick at the time, because you can recognize it . . . when you feel the same way.[17]

Despite regional and cultural differences, working side by side with Nevadans and competing in local sports events helped to close the gaps. Cultural barriers were almost always forgotten when enrollees and residents put their lives on the line fighting range fires. CCC firefighters protected human lives, livestock, and structures on forest- and rangelands for nearly a decade. The CCC labor force was an invaluable resource to federal land managers and civilian fire crews. Former forest ranger Archie Murchie, responsible for fire management in five western states including Nevada (U.S. Forest Service, Region 4), compared CCC crews with today's "hotshot" teams:

> They were awfully good fire crews. Every man knew his position, and they had their own foremen and their own straw bosses. . . . And twenty-five-man CCC crews could do more work than fifty pick-up men. Today's Indian hot-shot crews could probably put out as much work in a day as the CCC boys, but the recuperative power of the CCC boys . . . You could work their tails into the ground, but you give them plenty to eat and a night's sleep and they were ready to go the next day. I never saw a *tougher* bunch of men. . . . They weren't great big kids, but they were well built, and they had more endurance and recuperative power than any bunch of fire fighters that I have ever run across. And I'll call them men because they *were* men, even though they were boys.[18]

Socializing and Community Events

The CCC boys were better accepted in some communities than others. Camp Panaca CCC educational adviser Elmer Randall discussed how he kept the men under control:

> I don't think most of the locals thought too much of the boys. They were afraid of them. As an educational adviser, I had to take some pretty strong measures against them. These kids get smart with a guy down there [in town], and we wouldn't let him go on a recreation trip. Well, the town people wouldn't want their daughters going out with these uneducated ruffians, and that's where some of the friction came in. But I was big enough to handle them. If you're big enough to kick the hell out of them, you don't have to [laughter]. They were under my thumb. I had the backing of the first and second officers around there.[19]

CCC officials did their best to promote public relations. One of the best ways to become acquainted with the communities was to hold a yearly open house, usually in commemoration of the CCC program's anniversary. During these events, local citizens were familiarized with the CCC mission, the young men, and plans for improvements in their communities. Open houses were always well attended. Camp cooks worked for days preparing food for hundreds of guests in addition to a company of two hundred or more men. Guests were well entertained. Planned events at Camp Sadlers Ranch's fourth anniversary celebration included a baseball game between the enrollees and a Eureka team, swimming in a nearby warm lake, horseback riding, and dancing in the recreation hall.[20]

To maintain good morale and fend off boredom, educational advisers often created "pep clubs." Camp Sunnyside's "boarders" arranged dances and other social activities. Under the direction of education adviser L. R. Scott, one community event was a "minstrel" show within the setting of a jailhouse. The camp quartet and orchestra trained regularly and provided entertainment in camp and at town events.[21]

CCC camps sponsored regular dances and mixers, oftentimes with the assistance of local businesses and service clubs. Dancing was very popular with the young men, who were eager to have fun and to find, if lucky, female companionship on weekends. Town newspapers obligingly helped promote CCC-sponsored fund-raisers and activities, and local businesses offered their facilities for these functions. For example, a dance organized by the CCC and the Eureka Orchestra was held at the Eureka Hotel. In Hawthorne, benefit dances were often held at the Hawthorne K. P. Hall. Local musicians, such as Stella's Harmony Sextet, played "new dance hits and regular snappy numbers." As a matter of practice, women were admitted free of charge.[22]

Marshall Crawford, a Yerington resident who served at Camp Hawthorne, said that the five dollars a month he kept was usually adequate for the modest recreation available to the men:

> I made twenty-one dollars [actually thirty dollars] a month . . . and they gave me five dollars. Well, that was my spending money, but it was enough. I didn't have any place to go or much to do. We went to Hawthorne a time or two, walked around the streets. . . . They had Saturday night dances, and we did go to those dances. . . . It cost us a dollar to go to the dance. . . . The local girls were all turned out, and most of them would dance with us, but I guess not all of them would.[23]

Saturday night dances were not only fun but also profitable. Proceeds paid for athletic supplies and uniforms. In the city of Reno, however, enrollees were more apt to patronize local dance establishments such as the Tavern and Tony's El Patio rather than organize community events. Conversely, in small rural areas such as Paradise Valley, social events were far more challenging. Edna Timmons recalled how enrollees looked forward to the dances: "They never missed a dance in Paradise. There would be ten girls for forty boys, but . . . that was the fun of it. . . . They didn't care whether you were married or ten years old. If you wanted to dance, they liked to dance."[24]

Theatrical plays were equally popular in communities such as Hawthorne. Several enrollees displayed their talents by participating in a mirth-provoking mystery play, *The Haunted House,* that amused a packed house for more than two hours. The amateur thespians—composed of a group of CCC enrollees, naval depot employees, and town residents—later took their act to Tonopah.[25] In smaller towns, entertainment was understandably more meager. In Paradise Valley, the boys looked forward to free movies shown weekly at the Paradise Hotel.[26]

Several ranchers recalled the boys coming to visit, have lunch, and ride horses. Enrollees from Camp Reno liked to hang out at the Bartley Ranch on their days off. Elsewhere, Camp Sunnyside boys liked to ride horses at the Hendricks Ranch, south of Lund. Their eagerness to learn made up for their lack of riding experience. The Hendricks family was extremely grateful when men from the neighboring CCC camp helped them escape a fire that destroyed their ranch house in 1935. According to Dixie Whipple, "They were the first ones at the scene."[27]

CCC enrollees in camps near towns usually adjusted more easily to their surroundings. CCC and federal officials soon learned about the effect of isolation on camp morale. In extreme rural settings, army and government officials tried to compensate by improving gym facilities, promoting intercamp sports competitions, and granting extended leave at scheduled intervals. Nonetheless, enrollees in Camp Sheldon at the Sheldon Antelope Refuge on the Nevada-Oregon border seldom made it into town due to the remote location and severely rutted roads.[28]

It was not uncommon for enrollees to make long-lasting friendships. Some of the men even married local girls. One better-known union was between Wendell Wheat of Camp Newlands and Great Basin anthropologist Margaret (Hatton) Wheat of Fallon. The Wheats remained in Nevada, and Wendell assisted his wife during her seminal ethnographic study of the Stillwater Paiute people.[29] Enrollee Calvin Cushing from Illinois recalled that two of his Camp Hubbard Ranch buddies married local girls from Wells, Nevada, and Twin Falls, Idaho. Cushing enjoyed the wide-open spaces and would also have remained in Nevada if his mother had not needed him in Missouri. Despite stories of families hiding their daughters when the CCC boys came to town, Cushing dated the daughter of a Texaco gas station owner and was well liked by her family. Cushing also gained the trust of his foreman, gold miner Joe Mellan:

> He was one of our camp field managers, and he lived in Tonopah, Nevada. On weekends he would . . . work on a gold mine that he had there. I got acquainted with him and I did some odd jobs for him. He asked me if I wanted cash or bonds or stock, and I figured we'll see what the stock would do. So he gave me two hundred shares of Mellan gold mine stock. . . . When I left Nevada, I never heard any more from Mr. Mellan until after the war, and I found out that he was deceased, but his wife wrote and said that they had litigation against the government for . . . [taking] over the gold mine that they had at Tonopah . . . on Nellis Air Force Range. It's sitting there. Nobody is working it.[30]

Sports Competitions

Group sports not only were good for morale but also encouraged interaction between enrollees and the local ball teams. More than any other activity, sports competitions were the avenue through which new friendships were made. The games were always lively. Enrollees around the country played a lot of baseball, and many of the players were quite talented. Some were so good that professional scouts were known to select CCC enrollees to fill vacancies in the American and National Leagues.[31] Uniforms with the

The Camp Newlands baseball team won the state CCC championship in 1936. Pictured in top row *(from left to right):* enrollees Baker, Lumos, Goone, McGinnis, Yates, Schamp, Franzier, Cooper, Wonderly, and Curd; bottom row: Stien, Lore, Earnest, Gill, Brooke, Negil, and Worth. Courtesy Ralph Hash

Baseball players don the Camp Hubbard Ranch uniform. Courtesy Calvin Cushing

camp name were commonly worn, and baseball diamonds became the heart of most camps. The Camp Newlands baseball team, predominantly composed of Missouri boys, went on to win the state championships against other CCC and state league teams in the summer of 1936. The Camp Newlands team continued their winning streak and made it to the CCC interstate competitions in Sacramento.[32]

CCC ball teams regularly competed with town teams. Newspapers reported the best plays, the names of players, and the excitement of each game. Some of the most heated competitions occurred between enrollees and Ely ball teams. Sparks flew when local teams lost to the boys. One upset came when the Indian Springs Braves "trounced" the highly touted team from McGill. During the next season, in 1937, the Braves team defeated the Wilson-Bates Outfit and the Nevada Northern Rails, placing them at the top of the White Pine County League. They set a new record for runs made by a single team when they "swamped" the Elks under a torrent of thirty-four runs. Local teams eagerly prepared for the next game: "A picked Ely softball team will meet the widely self-heralded Indian Springs CCC team tomorrow at the city park. . . . This will be the first time that an Ely team has been chosen beforehand to meet the 3C club and advance dope shows that the locals will be out for blood and all indications point toward a real grudge game."[33] Disappointingly, the outcome of this game was not covered by the Ely newspapers.

The Indian Spring boys also staged boxing and wrestling competitions. Enrollees received permission from district headquarters to feature a boxing show to raise funds for their educational facility. The show included twenty four fast rounds of boxing accompanied by special "spicy musical numbers." The Ely community also helped promote boxing events. The American Legion donated its hall for the match, and tickets were sold at the Steptoe Drug Company and by other merchants. Boxing was also popular in the small town of Hawthorne, and the CCC boys heightened the competition. A New Year's celebration in 1933 included a boxing match sponsored by the American Legion and Veterans of Foreign Wars. Featured boxers were the "highly touted Pugs" from the CCC camp, the "Marine Leather Slingers," and a Native American boxing champion from Schurz.[34]

Boxing was also a means to settle disputes among the men. The sport was highly popular across the country and taught at Boys' Clubs for self-defense as well as recreation. Camp Hawthorne enrollee Bud Wilbur ex-

Boxing was a popular pastime at CCC camps. Novice boxers spar at Camp Indian Springs, west of Ely. Courtesy Rex Hines

plained the significance of boxing during that era and how it was used to keep harmony in camp:

> The Golden Gloves Program was very, very popular in the United States at the time . . . in fact, throughout the world. And, you're talking about men like Max Baer and Gene Tuney and Jack Johnson and Joe Lewis and [Rocky] Graciano and all those big-time boxers that made boxing what it is today. . . . The commanding officer had a pair of boxing gloves, and he kept his finger on the pulse of the camp. If there were people who were having problems with one another, he would get them both together, put them in a boxing ring, put the gloves on and say, "Let 'er go." That would take care of a lot of animosity. If there were belligerent types—and we had a couple in our camp—the first sergeant was an excellent boxer, and he would take them on and get their attention real quick.[35]

In their quest to fend off boredom, CCC and agency officials supplied each camp with physical fitness equipment and games and encouraged social activities. In some places, less traditional forms of entertainment were available, like dancing lessons. Las Vegas resident Terese Thomas, assisted by teenage girls from Boulder City, taught ballroom dancing to the CCC boys so that they could participate in town dances. Thomas recalled: "So many of them said they didn't know how to dance."[36]

Some camps had special sports facilities. Camp Quinn River constructed a six-hole golf course that was the pride of the camp. Other camps, including Indian Springs and Westgate, had swimming pools used by enrollees and visitors alike. Most camps were equipped with Ping-Pong tables, horseshoes, and various table games. Skills taught in camp included leather working, photography, and carpentry. Current movies rotated among the camps and were shown weekly on 35mm projectors. For the more studious, camp libraries were stocked with books and newspapers from the company's hometown. Through grants, the WPA extended library services by distributing books to isolated communities as well as CCC camps.[37]

Today, most CCC alumni have lasting impressions of the softball tournaments, boxing matches, driving lessons, and friends that they made in camp and in nearby communities as well. Enrollees clearly benefited from Nevada's small-town hospitality during their stays.

PART II

CCC Contributions and the Legacy Left Behind

5

Rehabilitating the Public Domain

The Grazing Service CCC Program

The Civilian Conservation Corps operated fifty-nine main camps in Nevada, many simultaneously. While some programs were short-lived, others such as Camps Muddy River and Newlands operated seasonally or year-round for most of the CCC's nine-year existence.

The placement and longevity of each camp was generally influenced by the needs of a particular region as well as the political agendas of the advisory boards and federal agencies. The nature of the work was shaped by the natural and affected environment. Work plans were developed by the Division of Grazing and local advisory boards.

For example, with the lack of surface water near Battle Mountain, Camp Mill Creek concentrated on building windmills and sinking wells so that formerly unusable land could be grazed. Elsewhere, camps at Tuscarora west of the Independence Range and Hubbard Ranch east of Jarbidge Wilderness were bordered by high mountains. Here, attention was focused on building earthen dams and reservoirs to store snowmelt for the dry summer months.

The government agencies that supervised CCC projects varied from state to states. In Nevada, the U.S. Department of the Interior (USDI) served as the umbrella agency for the following departments and bureaus: Department of Grazing/Grazing Service (now the Bureau of Land Management), Bureau of Reclamation, the National Park Service, and Biological Survey/Fish and Wildlife Service.

Division of Grazing/Grazing Service

The Division of Grazing (Grazing Service as of 1939) operated the greatest number of CCC programs in the state. There were several reasons for this. First of all, Nevada has the largest public domain (nonallocated federal acreage) of any of the forty-eight contiguous states. With little trouble, Nevada's elected officials and stockmen easily persuaded national CCC officials to approve requests for several new grazing camps, notwithstanding national CCC program budget cuts. Second, following passage of the Taylor Grazing Act of 1934, a large workforce was needed to implement its ambitious provisions. Even with CCC assistance, the amount of work needing to be accomplished was unparalleled.

With the federal mandate and a free CCC workforce, there was no time to waste. Secretary of Interior Harold Ickes acknowledged that decades of overgrazing largely contributed to the progressive deterioration of the land. More palatable forage plants were being displaced by species of little worth. Without protection, Ickes feared that grassy rangelands would be replaced by acres of desert land.[1]

Essentially, the Division of Grazing was created to administer the Taylor Grazing Act. Secretary Ickes laid out the main programs mandated by the act: extensive water development to permit an even distribution of livestock, eradication of rodents that compete for feed resources, construction of drift fences to allow for more effective range management, construction of truck trails to deliver feed or water to stock in distress or to transport stock between ranges, eradication of noxious weeds, and erosion control.[2]

The Taylor Grazing Act was designed to salvage both the livestock industry and the environment. Despite its good intentions, the grazing program was not immediately embraced and created its share of controversy. As intended, not all stockmen would gain from its provisions. Itinerant ranchers were put out of business, whereas those with established ties to the land received grazing permits. Permitted stockmen were charged a per-head fee dedicated to range improvements. Of the new fee, 50 percent went to the state grazing boards and 25 percent was returned to local grazing boards.[3] Frequently, both state and local fees were earmarked for supplies and materials for CCC projects. This proved to be a win-win situation, as ranchers reaped the benefit of free CCC labor and enrollees received a small wage, technical training, shelter, and three meals a day.

The amount of CCC work on Nevada's public domain was impressive by any standard. In Nevada alone, CCC officials estimated that $13,392,000 was expended on the grazing program during its first five years.[4] By the end of the program in 1942, the CCC Grazing Service's program had constructed 15 miles of pipelines for spring development, 26 large impounding or diversion dams, 260 miles of fence, 60 cattle guards, almost 2,000 miles of truck trails, and 800 permanent and temporary check dams. In addition,

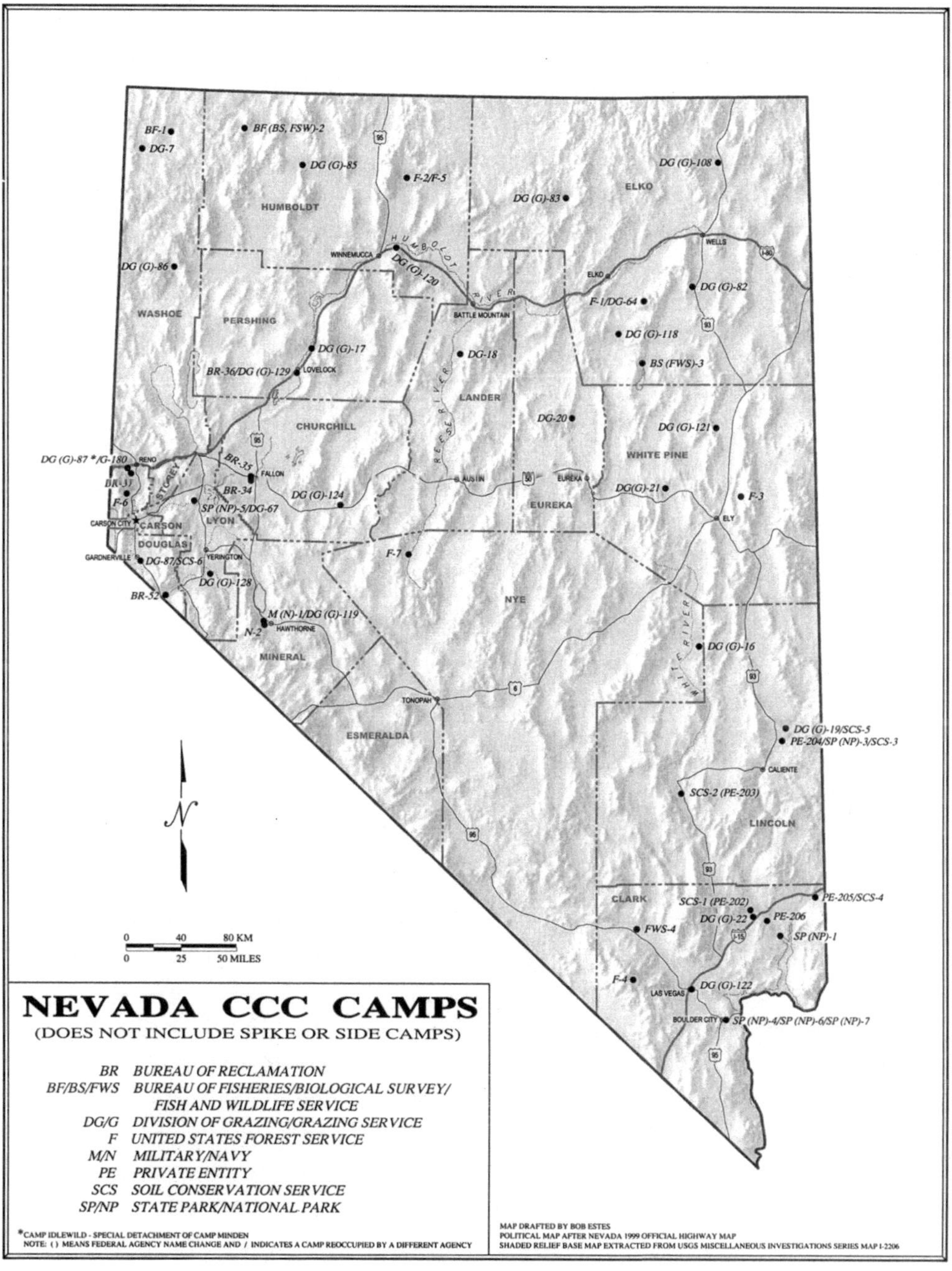

CCC Map of Nevada Camps. Courtesy Bob Estes

approximately 80 miles of stock driveways were marked, more than 30,000 acres of poisonous and noxious weeds were eradicated, and crickets and grasshoppers were fought on more than 100,000 acres. CCC firefighting was a major endeavor and man-days exceeded 10,000 per year.[5]

As a result of private and public collaboration, five grazing districts were established in Nevada during the CCC years. The districts were administered by local advisory boards once Congress granted them legal status in 1939. Farrington Carpenter was the first appointed director of the Grazing Service, followed by Richard H. Rutledge.[6] Lester R. Brooks was the first regional grazier for District 3, covering most of Nevada and northeastern California. Nevada's first regional improvement supervisor in charge of the CCC program was Chester R. Hunt. Range surveys were conducted from the division's drafting office at Camp Idlewild in Reno. Retired colonel Thomas Woodnut Miller, the first engineer inspector in charge of the CCC program, replaced Hunt as regional improvement supervisor in 1938.[7] Miller was an influential, charismatic figure who knew how to garner support for the grazing program. His conservative political orientation and militaristic views made him most suitable for the job.

Once new grazing districts were established, there were few losers beyond the handful of ranchers in rural areas. Stockmen working outside of grazing-district boundaries were livid when several existing CCC camps were terminated. This decision meant that camps such as Camp Sadlers Ranch (Eureka County), Camp Indian Springs (White Pine County), and Camp Sunnyside (northern Nye County) would be closed.

Despite public outcries, there was little recourse—at least not immediately. Eureka-area ranchers sent stern letters to U.S. Congressman Scrugham and Senator McCarran. The stockmen received conciliatory responses; however, instructions from Washington, D.C., were clear—CCC camps would henceforth be confined to counties with established grazing districts.[8] At first, only Elko, Humboldt, and Washoe Counties qualified, although Nevada's representatives promised to explore the prospect of new grazing districts with the proper authorities.[9] Their efforts eventually paid off. Intensive lobbying resulted in the creation of the Ely Grazing District. Thus, two of the closed camps, Sunnyside and Indian Springs, were reestablished.

Nevada grazing officials set overly optimistic goals and hoped to rehabilitate 34 million acres of public lands in grazing districts by 1938.[10] Even with CCC assistance, officials knew that it would take years to achieve even satisfactory results on depleted rangelands. The massive rehabilitation effort was hampered by the extremely remote and rugged nature of Nevada's public domain. National CCC director Robert Fechner publicized a 1936 Division of Grazing report outlining the challenges:

> A survey of the accomplishments of the CCC camps reads like a tale of frontier days rather than a record of work under present day conditions. To complete some of these projects the enrollees have had to carry sand, cement, pipes and other necessary equipment over mountain trails. Miles of telephone lines have been constructed in sections of the West which theretofore had not known this form of communication. Roads had been built where before there had been only cow paths. Water has been brought to this drought-stricken, denuded range country. It is pioneer work in rehabilitating the public domain, and it is pioneer work in terms of men.[11]

Although the Taylor Grazing Act brought new controls to the range, the number of permitted livestock remained questionably high. To illustrate, the *Congressional Record* reported a total of 1,978 permits issued in 1939 allowing 1,366,456 head of livestock (269,543 cattle, 13,954 horses, 1,081,113 sheep, and 1,846 goats) to graze the public domain.[12]

In Nevada, twenty-six CCC grazing camps operated at various times and locations during the life of the program. Main or parent camps were usually established on or near large ranching outfits such as Sadlers Ranch, Dunphy Ranch, Quinn River Ranch, Moorman Ranch, Board Corrals, Dressler Ranch, Sunnyside Ranch, and Delmues Ranch. The army frequently established one or more subsidiary camps, called side or spike camps, when the necessary work was too far from the main camps for a daily commute. Up to fifty men, including cooks, foremen, and one or two army officers, were detailed to the temporary encampments. Camps located in high-elevation areas with cold climates were operated seasonally by necessity. Nonetheless, summer camps such as Tuscarora had a complete camp staff.

Camp superintendents were overseers of all work projects in the field. Superintendent positions were often political appointees paid by a federal agency. The superintendents hired local experienced men or foremen from nearby communities. In turn, foremen trained the inexperienced enrollees and supervised specific tasks, such as carpentry, masonry, or road building. Although political connections often influenced who was hired, local residents complained if outsiders were selected. The concerns of the local citi-

The CCC found it practical to establish small temporary camps close to the work. Here, Camp Mill Creek enrollees pose at the sign to a spike camp at Dunphy Ranch, ca. 1936. Photos by William R. Black from the collection of Mr. and Mrs. Robert G. Harmon

The Camp Twin Bridges staff included *(from left to right)* education adviser Aland Forgeon, commanding officers Campbell and Olijsgewski, and "Doc" Anderson, ca. 1939. Courtesy Joseph Chmielewski

zenry prompted Senator McCarran to pressure Improvement Supervisor Thomas Miller into considering local men first:

> Sometime ago, I recommended Mr. Blaire Oakey of Yerington, Nevada, a graduate of the University of Nevada, for superintendent of the grazing camp at Tuscarora. Mr. Oakey comes to me highly recommended by all of the members of the faculty of the University of Nevada. . . . He knows the livestock business from a practical standpoint as well as from a theoretical standpoint in that he was raised in the business. . . . There seems to be a persistency to bring in those from outside and I am going to take the position that, so long as there is a place to fill, Nevada residents and those who belong to Nevada should be given the positions as against outsiders.[13]

The types of work performed and experiences on the range are best described by enrollees. Bud Wilbur was assigned to the Camp Hawthorne grazing camp that replaced the former military camps at the ammunition depot. The following excerpt is from his oral history.

Vernard "Bud" Wilbur, Camp Hawthorne (DG/G-119)

I was born in Binghamton, New York, on October 11, 1919. . . . I was eighteen when I joined the CCC. . . . We were assigned to Company 3273 out of New York City. There were Jewish kids, Italian kids, Irish kids, and probably the best mix of nationalities that you could find. . . . It took us eight days to go from Camp Dix to Hawthorne, Nevada. For most of us who had never been outside of the city since we were born, there was a lot of amazement and wonderment at the things we saw. . . . We went to Chicago first. . . . We went through the great plains of Kansas and Colorado . . . into Utah, into the flat desert country. From Utah we cut back through to Reno. It was a beautiful site to see . . . nature and all of its beauty. It was sort of unmarred, and man hadn't messed with it too much. . . . In Reno, we just switched trains, and they pulled us down to Hawthorne, Nevada. . . . One of the big things . . . you'd never see in the eastern part of the county, they had a big *H* on the mountainside.

Teamwork was extremely important. And I think that's what the army had in mind when they . . . put us in barracks, military style—yes sir and no sir, left and right, shoes polished, clothes hung and buttoned the same way. You treat your fellow man the same way, because you never know what your next day of work is going to be and you had to pull together as a team. Quite often, if there was any difference in what was going on at that time about pulling your own weight, especially in a forest fire or range fire, you know, you could be in deep trouble in short order.

. . . We had what we called a kangaroo court. It was a court of your peers. . . . A good example is, if you were out doing a particular job, and this guy was laying down on the side of the road—didn't want to work, wasn't carrying his part of the load . . . —it would get back to the old man, and he would say, "Well, you hold a kangaroo court and take action." That was pretty rough, because the guy was being disciplined by the men that he worked with. You either followed through, or in many, many cases they went over the hill and went home—AWOL, absent without leave. In fact, most every CCC camp, I'm sure, had people that just weren't fit for it.

It was hard work, since we came from a city and weren't used to this type of work eight hours a day. . . . But they fed you well. . . . We graded roads. . . . We dug out a big reservoir about a mile above camp and firmed it all up with rocks and so forth, and then it was filled so that stockmen could use it for drinking water for cattle. . . . A reservoir for cattle was important because . . . the saline content of Walker Lake is totally unacceptable.

We used to dig cattle dips. Oh heck, they were probably five or six feet wide and maybe ten or fifteen yards long, and we dug them out and lined them up with different types of rock material. They would fill it up with water, and put a disinfectant in it, and run the cattle through there to kill ticks. The Rocky Mountain spotted fever tick was quite predominant at that time in the West. In fact, enrollees were inoculated, and for that particular type of shot you have to take it in the stomach. . . .

Some of it was pick-and-shovel work. A lot of it was pole-type work, especially on the barbwire, and hammering with staples. And, if you will, using the terminology of the Marine Corps, "grunt-type labor."

We learned desert survival, about rattlesnakes . . . from the foreman. His name was Mr. Ashbaugh, a young man about twenty-five years old. . . . But he was a graduate from Colorado A&M. And he used to tell us the stories about him going to college, and what he had learned on the range from being in Colorado.

What did the camp leave behind for Nevada? I just think all the miles of range with the graded roads . . . allowed the ranchers access to get to places where they were never able to get into before. . . . All the cattle guards that they put across the roads—they are still there today. . . . There were no cattle guards when we started, not that I remember. And all the fencing. . . .

I was at Hawthorne about sixteen months. Oh, I think western people are some of the finest people in the world. They are about as down-to-earth as you can get.

Incidentally, we had to go through the naval base to get to our camp in Hawthorne, drive through there with our military trucks. It was guarded by the United States Marines. At that time, that was a beautiful base. It was painted nice and white; the GIs were sharp and very memorable and envied by most of the CCC men. . . . Seeing that beautiful base, I wanted to be one of them. I served twenty-four years in the military.[14]

Range Improvements

General plans for range improvements were generated at the grazing district's Region 3 headquarters at Camp Idlewild in Reno. The detachment of Camp Minden housed a fifty-man staff that established range boundaries, drafted base maps, and compiled landownership records. They also helped determine the carrying capacity for allotments in newly established grazing districts.

Enrollees assigned to Camp Idlewild were fortunate for a variety of reasons. The camp was located on the Truckee River in Reno. There was no shortage of social activities in the "Biggest Little City." Furthermore, working at the drafting camp was considered a privilege, and enrollees were selected from outlying camps on the basis of "experience, education and character."[15] Not surprisingly, competition for a limited number of drafting positions was keen. Camp Idlewild enrollees received valuable technical training that increased their marketability. One CCC inspector reported that up to one-third of Camp Idlewild's enrollees accepted local employment during each six-month enrollment period.[16]

It is difficult to assess the real value of the CCC contribution to the public domain. District grazing records reflect hundreds of projects accomplished with CCC labor. By providing water and access, the CCC opened up vast expanses of rangelands that would be available for grazing. But before reservoirs, corrals, and spring improvements could be constructed, thousands of miles of roads would have to be built. Consequently, the Division of Grazing referred to truck trails as the "daddy of them all."[17] Once built, the light-duty twenty-foot-wide roads allowed stockmen to transport their herds between winter and summer ranges, provide feed and water to ani-

A foreman from Camp Muddy River grades Whitney Ranch Road through the lower Moapa Valley. Courtesy Special Collections, University of Nevada, Reno Library

mals in distress, and fight range fires on remote mountaintops. Many of the trails were partially dug by hand with a pick and a shovel. Terrain permitting, some early grading machines were also utilized.

Improving and protecting natural springs was also high on the list of priorities. Livestock, particularly sheep, are notorious for trampling down springs, so exclosures were built around spring heads to prevent further damage. Reservoirs with earthen, concrete, and rock dams were constructed to impound water that would otherwise be absorbed into the ground. Many reservoirs were dug using horse-drawn Fresno Scrapers. Most of these small to large reservoirs remain in use. Ranch owner Marla Griswold still refers to the two earthen reservoirs in the foothills west of her property as the "lifeblood" of the Hubbard Ranch.[18]

In extremely arid regions, large water tanks were installed to store water for short-term use. Water was released into troughs when herds were driven onto a range. Since many central Nevada basins lack springs, lakes, and streams, scores of wells were dug to access groundwater. Windmill crews installed hundreds of wells, windmills, and troughs in arid valleys across central Nevada.

Stockmen knew that additional rangelands could be grazed if water was available. A Camp Mill Creek crew is shown drilling one of many wells near Battle Mountain, ca. 1936. William R. Black Collection, courtesy of Mr. and Mrs. Robert G. Harmon

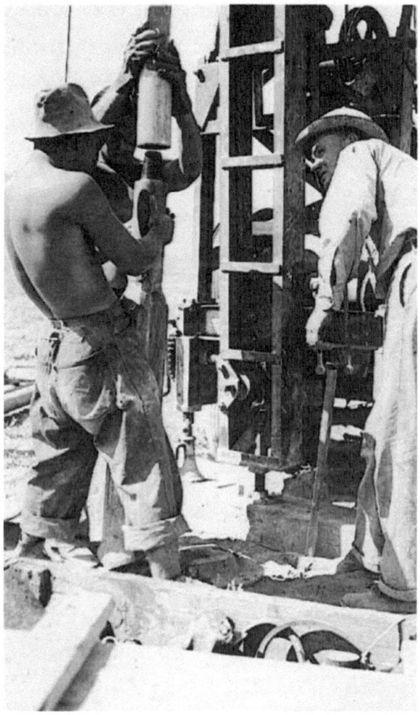

A windmill, redwood water tank, and trough were installed at a new well site near Battle Mountain, ca. 1936. William R. Black Collection, courtesy of Mr. and Mrs. Robert G. Harmon

The Taylor Grazing Act essentially fenced the remainder of the untamed West. Newly created boundaries for grazing districts and individual allotments created a need for miles of drift fences and cattle guards. Drift fences made of juniper posts and barbed wire prevented cattle from straying into adjacent allotments. Consequently, thousands of juniper trees were cut for fence posts. However, in rocky terrain, other fencing was sometimes employed. One impressive segment of rock fence, nicknamed "the Chinese Wall," was built over Mount Como in the Pinenut Range, to separate Mason Valley and Carson Valley Ranges.[19] Contrary to initial impressions, the CCC was actually responsible for its construction. The Grazing Service chose to use available rock to avoid hauling juniper posts and wire to the high peak.[20] Impressed by the degree of difficulty, a local newspaper reported on the 1.5-mile-long rock wall built by a Camp Minden spike camp:

> A . . . group of boys [is] now engaged in building a drift fence from the northern extremes of the Pinenut Range to a point near Wellington. . . . The fence has been completed to the high ridge of Como peak. Along the top of this peak it was necessary to build a stone fence because of the rocky character of the region. To build the fence up this steep mountain, CCC boys carried posts and wire, a job of extreme physical difficulty. At the south slope of the mountain, a temporary road is now being built to transport material as near to the line of the fence as possible.[21]

The Grazing Service inspecting a Smith Valley cattle guard built by Camp Mason Valley, 1940. Courtesy Bureau of Land Management, Carson City Field Office

Camp Minden spike camp built this rock drift fence over the crest of Mount Como in the Pinenut Range. For years, historians mistakenly coined it the "Chinese Wall" (1985 photo). Courtesy R. T. King (UNOHP)

Camp Cherry Creek enrollees chopped down countless juniper trees to fence new grazing allotments in their district. Courtesy Special Collections, University of Nevada, Reno Library

Massive insect infestations added to the problems on the range and plagued ranchers throughout the 1930s. "Cricket crews" consisting of local men and enrollees worked tirelessly to control Mormon crickets. A particularly bad year was 1936 when crickets ravaged a forty thousand–square-mile area in three Nevada counties.[22] To the dismay of stockmen, the plant-eating insects consumed every blade of grass in their paths and robbed the range of its sparse vegetation.

Several successful methods were employed to keep the insects at bay. Cricket crews often dug extensive trenches lined with upright tin sheeting to block the relentless insects. When the insects reached the tin wall and slipped into the trenches, they were doused with oil and set afire. Chemicals such as arsenic in powder form were used to dust young crickets. This deadly mixture was replaced with a fluo-silicate mixed with bran after enrollees became sick and birds and livestock were affected. After a few such incidents, CCC boys were no longer allowed to dust crickets.[23]

Enrollees were the principal firefighters on public domain and Forest Service lands. Grazing camp crews frequently worked alongside Forest Service crews, Native Americans, and civilian crews. Jurisdictional boundaries rarely stood in the way. Although brush fires were usually covered by the nearest camp, in larger incidents, calls for help went out to surrounding camps. In one instance, seventy-five men from Camp Reno came to the aid of several California Grazing Service camps attempting to contain an eight hundred–acre fire in Sierraville, California, in 1936.[24] During a four thousand–acre fire in rough terrain at Fort Sage Mountain, enrollees from Camps Gerlach, Mason Valley, Minden, Idlewild, Westgate, Fish Springs Spike Camp (a Gerlach detachment), and Juniper Flats in Likely, California, responded to the 9.5-mile-long by 1-mile-wide blaze.[25] During a heavy fire season in 1940, nineteen camps in seven grazing districts of Nevada and California fought 173 fires within a five-month period between June and October. The Grazing Service reported that CCC camps in the two states expended twenty-two thousand "man hours" with a total cash outlay of $6 million. The CCC was further credited with saving $650,000 in property.[26]

After a series of severe fire years, lookout towers were constructed along the eastern Sierra front. One important tower was built at the summit of Mount Peavine overlooking the Truckee Meadows. From there, fire watchers could view the surrounding Plumas, Tahoe, and Mono National Forests and rangelands to the north and south of Reno. In the spirit of cooperation, the Forest Service supplied the lookout building and sleeping quarters, and the Grazing Service provided the workforce and supervision. However, the lookout tower could not be built until the CCC constructed a five-mile road from U.S. Highway 395 (six miles north of Reno) to the Peavine Summit. Although the original lookout tower has been replaced, the access road is still in use today.[27]

Pressure from elected representatives sometimes forced grazing officials to alter their work plans. This was the case in 1941 when enrollment was down and the program was being phased out. Regional grazier L. R. Brooks was understandably eager to complete projects already under way. At the request of the town of Wells, Senator McCarran asked local Grazing and Forest Service camps to build a twenty-two-mile road from Wells to a proposed ski jump at Angel Lake in the Ruby Mountains. Initially, Brooks was opposed to assigning CCC crews to the project and questioned the appropriateness of using grazing fees for purposes other than range improvements and fire control. To Brooks's dismay, he soon realized that the elected official would not be dissuaded. McCarran's response to Brooks was to get on board:

> I appreciate all you say in your letter and I realize that it is of vital importance that fire-breaks be established to eliminate the fire hazard in Clover Valley, but I cannot permit the Angel Lake project to go by the board. That project must go in and there isn't any use in trying to persuade me that it can't go in. . . . [B]y making a start we will give encouragement to the people of Wells. . . . So I want to assure you that I am behind this thing and that I am resolved to see it through and I want your resolution to be of the same nature, which I know it will be, eventually.[28]

The issue of dedicated funds was incidental by comparison to the use of enrollees for the national defense projects late in the CCC program. By now the War Department knew that U.S. involvement in World War II was imminent and that many of these young men would soon be inducted into military service. Defense-related training was purposely incorporated into most CCC programs. The CCC's changing focus created an outpouring of concern from citizens and government personnel who questioned the legitimacy of these actions. At first, CCC officials and rank-and-file army officers denied any changes in the CCC mission.

Despite the government's initial denials, military preparedness occurred gradually, beginning with the addition of fifteen minutes of marching and simple formations to the daily basic training program.[29] Next, a variety of military support skills were also incorporated into the educational curriculum. Training in skills essential to national defense, including auto mechanics and motor maintenance, radio operation, and truck driving, was taught at several grazing camps. At a 1941 CCC national defense conference at the Presidio in San Francisco, Improvement Supervisor Thomas Woodnut Miller openly discussed how grazing-camp enrollees were being trained in vocations useful to the war effort. By now, full-time radio schools had been established at Camps Minden and Las Vegas, a full-time automotive school was set up in Mason Valley, and a central repair shop was built in Reno. Other defense-related training included a carpentry shop at Camp Westgate and a school of engineering at the Camp Idlewild range survey headquarters.[30]

The CCC boys' special training was soon called into use. Following the attack on Pearl Harbor in December 1941, hundreds of CCC boys with ham radio training were reassigned. Superintendents at six grazing camps were ordered to release five hundred to six hundred men to state and local defense authorities for the purpose of patrolling or guarding defense plants, mines, mills, smelters, bridges, and power plants in strategic locations.[31] In no time, enrollees were hired by the defense industry or were inducted into military service. Only a handful of CCC grazing camps managed to stay in operation during the massive budget cuts that led to the demise of the CCC program during the summer of 1942.

Educational adviser Claude Chadwell taught basic education skills at Camp Gerlach until 1939. He and his family left Gerlach only to return to help his Japanese in-laws, disrupted by the war.

Claude Chadwell, Educational Adviser, Camp Gerlach

Before [the] CCC, I went to a teachers' college. . . . We went to some of the schools for practice teaching, they called it. . . . I held classes for the CCC fellows and taught them arithmetic, typing—just general things like that. . . . We had a specific reading room stocked with, maybe, five or six different newspapers and magazines, and we had an extensive library.

Education advisers could help them finish high school, but they wouldn't get any high school credit from what we offered there. It wasn't connected with the school system. They did this after work, usually in the evening. Of course, they had different days off and some worked different times.

Generally, on weekends we could go to town. Gerlach in 1937 was just about the same as it is today. Pretty small place. Well, I guess you could say it was one of the last of the old western cowboy towns really. Oh, it was quite different from Tennessee [laughter]. I liked it. I liked the country. I liked the desert.

There were two factions, I guess, at Gerlach—people [who] worked on a ranch . . . and then there was a gypsum plant just a few miles away. The two groups kept the town going. . . .

Gerlach had a movie theater. Usually there was a dance every weekend—Saturday night. The townspeople were glad to have us there, because I think it helped the town. The work was under the Department of Grazing, and they were out there building roads or trails or dams or cattle guards. . . . Fisk Reservoir [Squaw Creek Reservoir] is still there. I believe they built that.

I met my future wife through the baseball team. We were playing the Gerlach baseball team and her brother Roy and I became friends, and he introduced me. Oh, I think the town had a better team than we did.

When I left, the camp was still open. I don't know if it was two years: that was the maximum you were supposed to serve then, unless you had some special job, like I did, which meant I could have stayed longer. But that was just before the war, and I realized that the camps were going to be broken up, so I went back to Tennessee and then Mary and I got married. . . .

Then the war broke out, then her family was disrupted, so then we went back to Gerlach to take care of them. . . . You know, most of the Japanese, whether they were citizens or not, were displaced, depending on where they lived. And Gerlach, being close to the Southern Pacific Railroad, they felt that was a danger to the safety of the U.S. So, they [his wife's parents] had to move [to Reno]. . . . Of course, the children were natural-born citizens. They were allowed to stay in the town all right. . . . Her two brothers were in the army, and then her sisters were left there with the parents.[32]

6

Irrigating the Desert West

The Bureau of Reclamation's CCC Program

The Bureau of Reclamation was painfully aware of the deteriorated condition of the early reclamation projects that were authorized by the Reclamation Act of 1902. At a Western States Water Conference in July 1933, President Roosevelt and members of the Senate discussed the persistent droughts, neglected irrigation systems, and inadequate storage for downstream users. Without hesitation, the president pledged immediate aid from his public works program. Senator McCarran apprised the president of proposed developments on the Carson, Truckee, and Humboldt Rivers. McCarran "gathered the impression that the President does not favor development of new reclamation projects, but is very much in favor of perfecting existing projects. I believe that he is with us in Western development one hundred per cent."[1]

The Newlands Project (originally the Carson Truckee Project) is considered Nevada's greatest reclamation project. The Truckee-Carson Irrigation District has operated the irrigation system since 1926. By the 1930s, the Newlands Project needed to be enlarged and overhauled if Fallon farmers were to stay in business.[2] The bureau was also concerned with the efficiency of irrigation systems in the Pershing County Water Conservation District in Lovelock, the Washoe County Water Conservation District in Reno, and the Walker River Irrigation District in Yerington.[3]

By 1935, five Bureau of Reclamation CCC camps had been established to store water and enlarge and upgrade existing irrigation systems. Concerned farmers were relieved by the prospect of receiving federal help. After falling on hard times, few of them were able to repay their construction loans to the bureau, let alone maintain the canals and ditches that delivered water to their land. The Newlands Project had particularly serious problems. Poor drainage and alkaline fields hindered crops on lower Lahontan Valley farms. Saturated fields meant poor crop yields and net operating losses. Since farmers were unable to shoulder the costs of the improvements, the Civilian Conservation Corps was the answer to their prayers.

Camps Newlands and Carson River worked primarily in the Fallon and Fernley areas. While Camp Carson River concentrated on improving the spillway at Lahontan Dam, Camp Newlands took on downstream canals and ditches. Camp Newlands also provided the labor force for the Walker River Irrigation District system in Smith Valley. At Topaz Lake, the CCC constructed the levee along the east bank of the intake canal, adding an additional twenty thousand acre-feet of water storage. Camps Newlands and Reno also maintained a summer camp at Boca Dam where enrollees worked on the Truckee Storage Project—a Nevada and California joint undertaking.[4]

Rehabilitating Federal Reclamation Projects

The Newlands Project represents one of the first five sites selected for federal reclamation work following passage of the Reclamation Act of 1902.[5] The act encouraged farmers to settle and farm several regions of the arid West. Lured by the prospect of homesteading the land, hundreds of families

An abandoned ditch on Country Lane near Fernley's Farm District bears the Camp Carson River stamp (2003 photo). Photograph by Renée Corona Kolvet

Men from Camps Reno and Newlands worked on several ancillary projects at Boca Reservoir near Truckee, California. One of their tasks was to lay rock riprap along the reservoir outlet channel. Courtesy Nevada Historical Society

traveled to Fallon seeking favorable sites. Some families actually arrived before irrigation water was available in early 1906.[6] Lahontan Dam, Carson River Diversion Dam, and the Carson River Dam were built early in the century to store water for irrigation and to generate power. The Truckee Canal was built to transport needed Truckee River water from Derby Dam to the Lahontan system. A portion of Truckee Canal water was (and still is) delivered to Fernley's Farm District along the way.

After more than twenty-five years of operation, however, many of the early water-control and -conveyance structures had fallen into a state of disrepair, and existing storage had proven inadequate. In Lahontan Valley, the CCC built or completed new water conservation projects including the Sheckler Reservoir and the S-Canal Dam and regulating reservoir to store more water. They also renovated and enlarged portions of the thirty-two-mile-long Truckee Canal, built several earth- and rock-filled dikes to increase reservoir capacity, and lined the Lahontan Dam spillways with rock riprap to protect its banks. Camp Carson River enrollee Joseph Ruchty recalls the hard physical labor:

> My first job was out working on the [Lahontan] reservoir riprapping with rocks. . . . We just had to watch our hands so we didn't get them smashed. Riprapping is putting the rocks down on a . . . forty-five-degree angle. We started at the bottom with the . . . bigger boulders, as the anchorage, and then you . . . work your way upward . . . with the flattest side up. . . . They'd dump the truck, and then the rocks would slide down. We took the parts that we wanted and moved the other ones, but we couldn't pick them up because they're too big. Just used back labor to push them around. We had crowbars and shovels and sand. . . . Well . . . we always dramatize anything when you're going to B.S. and tell people how hard you worked, but we worked hard. . . . If you're accepting the wages, you accept the work. . . . So the money was going home to my mother. That's the main thing. It helped her.[7]

Enrollee Harry Norman also recalled the perils of laying riprap and working outside in the elements. He eventually figured out how to market his other skills so that he could work within the camp:

> We went out and riprapped on the dam, and that was out in the cold. One time a storm come up—an ice storm. We had storms in New York, but nothing where you could not stand outside. These pellets were unbelievable. I got under a tractor to get away from it. Finally I said, "Hey, that's stupid." I saw a cab open in one of the trucks. . . . [T]he noise was horrendous. . . . They must have been like golf balls. They put dents in the roof of that cab. I didn't like to do things that put me in a position of danger. I heard about the snakes under the rocks. . . . So I volunteered to maintain anything in the camp. . . . So I was going to be repairing anything in the shop.
>
> "What do you know"? [they asked].
>
> "What do I know? I'm a kid." But I can do anything, so they put me in charge of the kitchen. They had a drain in the kitchen. . . . [T]he water used to wash down into a regular drain on the floor, and it used to wash away the dirt all of the time, because nobody knew how to make cement.
>
> So I said, "OK, I'll fix that."
>
> So I went out and I read what I could find, anyplace. That's where I found the school. I thought that it was a college—it was so big and beautiful. . . . It was a high school. . . . So I read, and then . . . I made cement. . . . They thought it was a miracle. . . . [A]nd I learned to do plumbing.[8]

The CCC was mainly assigned to rehabilitation and maintenance work. The men dug new drains and cleaned weeds and debris from hundreds of miles of water-conveyance canals, laterals, and ditches. They upgraded others by lining them with concrete and rebuilt aging diversion gates, bridges, and culverts in the process. By creating new drains, they helped eliminate ongoing problems with saturated fields and bothersome mosquitoes.[9]

Rehabilitating canals required an extensive rodent abatement program, as burrowing compromised the ditches and destroyed crops. With technical guidance from the Biological Survey, CCC crews lined canal walls with concrete, spread poison-laced oats on fields, and set traps. Bothersome Piute ground squirrels posed a major problem for Fallon farmers. The Bureau of Reclamation hired wildlife biologist J. R. Alcorn to supervise CCC rodent crews from 1936 to 1939. Although farmers were pleased, Alcorn soon learned that exterminating rodents was extremely unpopular with the indigenous Northern Paiute people. At the time, Native Americans still hunted ground squirrels for food or to trade with "old-timers" at Pyramid Lake. Alcorn documented a confrontation he had with an irate chief who threatened to have him arrested for killing the coveted squirrels. His report also mentions his awe-struck crew: "Everything considered, it seemed best to stop operations. I summoned my ten C.C.C. assistants and we moved to another location to finish the day's work. Many of the boys, who were fresh from New York City, were much impressed by this first meeting with an Indian."[10]

Ralph Hash, Camp Newlands

When I enrolled in the CCC, I lived in Missouri. . . . [M]y father was a farmer in Iowa and was poor—started out in debt, never got out—when the Depression hit. So he finally gave up and moved the family to Missouri . . . and I finished out high school [in 1935]. The Depression was on and terribly bad throughout the Midwest. On top of that we had crop failure from two droughts . . . Early that fall or late summer . . . my father and another neighbor . . . hoboed into Canada. They hired out and worked the harvest in Canada's wheat fields. . . . So when I got out of school, I was taking care of the farm. I was the farmer then. I had an aunt who lived in Moberly, Missouri . . . and she'd heard about the CCC, so she told Mother. Mother thought it was a good idea. . . . I left in . . . early September 1935. . . . It was the greatest thing in the world for a bunch of young kids who had just left home, and a lot of the kids were from the city and in worse straits than we were as farmers. . . .

All of the men that we were working under in Fallon had previous experience working with irrigation and canals. . . . The reason they had us there was that irrigation system . . . the Newlands Project. . . . And it hadn't received a lot of maintenance, because they didn't have the help. The canals that carried the water were becoming overgrown with brush and willows, and the locks (where they stopped the water and diverted it out into a field) were all wooden and rotting out. So our job was to clean canals and, in some places, build new locks out of cement. I started out as a plain laborer out in the field. . . . We had crews. We had about eight-and-a-half-ton dump trucks assigned to us, and we had about ten men assigned to each truck. For a day's work, we'd load up in the morning and go out to wherever they were working at overhauling banks of the canals that carried water. Some of them had to be filled in with a little more sand and dirt. . . . [I]t was hauled and dumped. We didn't have such things as loaders then. We made do with a good old shovel. That's what I did for a while.

Then I heard a rumor around that there was an opening at the camp: they needed an orderly for the state men who lived in camp. Each had their own quarters and their own toilet, and they ate at the mess hall with the group, but they had their own table. The orderly's job was to clean their quarters, mop the floors, make their beds, change their linen, tidy up, and feed them all their meals. . . . Boy, I had a gravy train. I lucked out on that one. . . . I just dashed in and volunteered. . . . The others put in more or less an eight-hour day. . . . They say in the army, "never volunteer." . . . This one time it was a good idea.

They completely rebuilt some of those main canals that carried the water out of the Lahontan Reservoir to the various farms. . . . In fact, we had what they called a spike camp. We took thirty men from our main camp and moved them over to Mason. . . . They were attached to the Walker River Irrigation System. . . . The reason Lake Topaz is there is that it's another dammed-up lake. At the lower end of it, they had a drain and a cement canal built underground through a cut in the mountain. It dumped water into the carrying canals below. They had to completely clean that canal: it was getting so filled up with silt and debris and junk. Well, it was their job to get in during the off-season when the water was down.

Oh, we had a lot of experiences. . . . They had a terrible fire up in the Tahoe City area—a terrible fire. It was out of control, and they couldn't get enough Forest Service people in there fighting it. So they called into the various CCC camps for volunteers. Of course they called ours, and there was a whole bunch of guys who thought, "Oh, that's neat."

Twenty or thirty of them or more volunteered. So they loaded them in a truck and put them up there on the fire line. I guess after four or five days of fighting that, they finally got them home. You wouldn't catch any of them volunteering again.

. . . [W]e had one boy get killed. . . . He was working out on a canal. . . . These big willows and stuff they cut out of the canal, some of them had pretty good-sized roots on them and trunks. They'd hook this little tractor-crawler, Cletrack—the size of a D4 Cat, on them with a chain, and they were pulling them out, so they'd get all cleaned out of there. They had it hooked up to one and they were pulling—somehow at an angle up the bank—and the chain broke and flipped the Cletrack. It landed square on him. . . . So, he's the only fatality. . . . Well, that's the first time I'd been around a death. . . . Pretty hard to handle . . .

Another thing that happened that I'll never forget . . . I wandered downtown on a Saturday afternoon. I didn't know what a bar was. Well, Iowa was a blue state: there wasn't such a thing in Iowa. So I walked into this bar, and I looked around—pretty full, Saturday afternoon. Some fellow had been playing roulette and won a bundle of money—about two thousand bucks.

"Drinks on the house!"

A drink, what's that? I said, "Yes, that's good, I'll take one [a boilermaker]." I couldn't breathe. I thought I was going to die. . . . I never had another taste of alcohol the rest of the time I was in Fallon.

Of course, there was also dancing. I didn't know what dancing was. There wasn't such a thing back home, especially with a bunch of good Baptists, you know. A group . . . in Fallon started . . . an orchestra, and we would have a dance out at the camp. . . . [T]hat's where I learned how to dance. . . . Later years, like when we first came to Reno, that was one of the greatest things Reno had . . . Tony's El Patio Ballroom. . . . Every Saturday night, Tony had a real good orchestra, and then during the year they'd bring in a lot of big-name orchestras. We've danced to Guy Lombardo, Glenn Miller, you name it—they were all there at one time or another.

My folks were good Baptists and I had that instilled into me, and so I attended church. The first Sunday there, the service is over, and some lady in front of me and her daughter turn: "Ah, you have the most beautiful voice. Would you like to be in the choir?"

I said, "Ha, no."

See, but that's how I met Gladys. Her mother introduced us of course, and that was my first date. So Gladys was a very close friend of Peggy's [Margaret

Wheat], and she's the one who introduced me to Peggy. . . . We became close friends. . . . I met Peggy in Fallon, probably a month or two after I arrived.[11]

I enjoyed myself a lot there, because I've always been active in sports so I had a lot of time to spend playing basketball and softball. One time we played the Fernley town team. All those towns had town baseball teams, and they were pretty good teams. They scheduled a game for us in Fernley with the Virginia City town team. Oh, man, what a game that was. The star player . . . was Jake Lawlor. Lawlor Event Center at UNR is named for him. That's where Jake was from, and Gil Martin. In their younger days they were hellions. . . . They almost killed us in that game. . . . What a rough game that was because we weren't even comparable in size to them. . . . The refereeing wasn't very strict in those games, so anything went, you know. Oh, they slaughtered us.

We had another game—same thing. We played the Stewart Indian School. . . . [T]hose Indians had a good ball club. The school had a little old, small gymnasium; and the line where you're out of bounds was only about, at the most, two feet from where the seats were—the lower seats all around. Some of the younger gals, they'd try to trip us as we were going by. Anything went, you know. They slaughtered us, too. We didn't play them again. But it was still fun.

. . . I know of at least six fellows that stayed in Nevada and married locally. . . . I know at last three or four that stayed in Fallon. . . . Another fellow . . . was Newt Loomis. He married a local Fallon girl when he got out, and he was quite an athlete. . . . When he and his wife moved to Reno . . . he took up golf. When they established a golf course out here at Stead—years ago . . . —they hired Newt as a pro.

I wanted to stay here in Reno. Basically, one of the reasons I took the job here [at Nevada Auto Supply] was that my father had worked his heart out twelve or sixteen hours a day all his life, and he had nothing. . . . I'd rather have been a farmer . . . but I thought: "If I take a regular job, I can work eight hours a day and forget it, come home, and I got my paycheck [seventy dollars a month] . . ." I turned out all right.[12]

Other Reclamation Projects

Many projects at Camps Lovelock and Reno were similar in scope, albeit less extensive, to those at Camps Newlands and Carson River. Camp Lovelock enrollees assisted with various improvements to the Humboldt Project, irrigation systems that delivered water to 20,000 acres of farmland. Enrollees eventually cleaned and improved 110 miles of main-line canals, laterals, and drains in Lovelock Valley.[13]

Camp Lovelock enrollees cleaned ditches and replaced worn-out water-control structures and flumes. They also worked on ancillary construction jobs during the final stage of construction of the Rye Patch Dam and Reservoir. The dam was built to store additional Humboldt River water. Water was distributed to farms by the Pershing County Water Conservation District. Enrollees learned to do finishing work and constructed the parapet walls and curbing on the roadway over the Rye Patch earthen embankment. The CCC work was performed outside of the main construction contract and was considered an indirect cost to the Humboldt Project. Other Rye Patch ancillary tasks included constructing a 1.25-mile telephone line from the Bell Telephone tie-in to the government office, clearing acres of brush in and around the reservoir, and riprapping the spillway slope. The CCC boys received excellent on-the-job training at Rye Patch Dam. An assistant engineer for the Bureau of Reclamation documented their progress:

> The opportunity to assist in the production of a high-class piece of construction, the variety and novelty of the various operations, the steady and orderly progress of the work from day to day, and the chance to learn from experienced inspectors, foremen, and skilled workmen all contributed to enhance the interest and enlist the cooperation of the enrollees to an unusual degree. The service of training and experience thus rendered to these willing young men was no small part of the public benefit accruing from this work project.[14]

In Reno, the Washoe County Water Conservation District's irrigation system had been ravaged by recent floods on the Truckee River. Camp Reno enrollees cleared logs and debris and placed rock riprap along eroded banks of the river. They also reconstructed several aging diversion dams and consolidated numerous water channels.[15] In the Truckee Meadows alone, the CCC cleared and repaired more than 200 miles of ditches.[16]

Camp Reno and Camp Newlands enrollees worked on ancillary tasks associated with the construction of Boca Dam and the Truckee Storage Project. The Bureau of Reclamation was responsible for the finishing work and brought in CCC crews to do most of it. Enrollees upgraded the surrounding road systems, and constructed two weir- and stream-gauging stations on the Little Truckee River. They also placed riprap on spillway banks and tunnel outlet channels and were responsible for building the rock-masonry parapet and timber-rail curb wall across the top of the dam.[17]

Camp Lovelock enrollees built the parapet wall and laid riprap over the earthen slope of Rye Patch Dam in 1938. Courtesy Pershing County Water Conservation District

There were valuable skills to be learned while working on dams. Pictured are enrollees compacting backfill behind the parapet wall at Rye Patch Dam in 1938. Courtesy Pershing County Water Conservation District

The CCC never intended to compete with union labor on large construction projects, although certain assignments at Boca Reservoir overstepped the established boundaries. Such was the case in August 1937 during a well-publicized labor strike. Boca Tunnel and Construction Workers from Local no. 402 angrily complained to the Department of Labor and the Bureau of Reclamation's commissioner when CCC workers were ordered to cross picket lines against their will. Enrollees assumed the union contractor's duties including jackhammer work, sloping, and bulldozing around the dam.[18] Union workers, holding out for an increase in the minimum hourly wage, were understandably resentful. Most of the men had families to support and could not compete with enrollees who worked for a dollar a day. The strike was covered by regional newspapers including the August 23, 1937 issue of the *Sacramento Bee*. Widespread attention helped to settle the strike. Fortunately, the union men were back on the job before the CCC got on the wrong side of organized labor.

Aside from a brush with the union, relatively few problems occurred at Nevada's Bureau of Reclamation camps. One exception was a highly publicized strike at Camp Reno. To the embarrassment of the army, the food and work strike was immediately brought to the attention of Nevada's elected representatives. The national CCC director ordered a special investigation of the cause of the strike that shut down work for several days. On November 30, 1936, the story hit local and national newspapers, including the *Los Angeles Times*. News of the strike enraged Congressman Scrugham who demanded immediate help from high-ranking officers at the Ninth Army Corps Area headquarters.[19]

Investigators attributed the turmoil to recurrent problems between the commanding officer, Captain Mansfield; the foremen (LEMs); and enrollees. Apparently, food selection was a major culprit. The men complained about the unpalatable meals and demanded more chicken and less starch. It seems, however, that the enrollees' late-night habits were the root of the problem. On several occasions, problem individuals failed to arrive at the mess hall within twenty minutes of the morning whistle. After several occurrences, the latecomers found the mess-hall doors locked and went without breakfast. The camp commander blamed the event on "too much Reno." Captain Mansfield argued that although a few men had missed meals, the entire company had gained weight while at his camp.[20] The problem was resolved after the ringleaders were dishonorably discharged and sent back to

The headline read, "Striking CCC Recruits Will Be Sent to N.Y. Home." The December 1, 1936, *Nevada State Journal* described the strikers' hands as "upraised in a mock Communist salute." Courtesy Nevada Historical Society

New York and the commanding officer was replaced. It was not long before the incident was forgotten and the men returned to work.

A few years would pass before Nevada's Bureau of Reclamation camps would again make the national news. But this time, they were recognized for their positive actions. During the CCC's final years, national security was on the minds of most Americans. CCC camps around the country were ordered to assist state and local defense authorities in protecting the homeland. When a U.S. Army Flying Fortress bomber crashed in the Trinity Mountains near Lovelock in 1941, a CCC road crew working nearby was the first to arrive at the scene.[21] Enrollees were distracted by the sounds of a plane in distress—the gunned motors followed by a nosedive and a deafening explosion that killed eight army fliers. Equipped with ham radios with statewide shortwave transmission, the crew sent an urgent radio message to Col. F. C. Nelson at McClellan Field in Sacramento. The men were ordered to stand guard at the sensitive crash scene. They had no way of knowing that the bomber was carrying confidential instrumentation during a time of national high alert. Later, the Lovelock crew received commendation for their judicious response.

Although the Bureau of Reclamation program was not the largest recipient of CCC support, its undertakings remain visible and important components of agricultural areas around the state. In the fast-growing areas of Reno and Fernley, lateral canals and ditches that once delivered water to farms have been replaced by housing subdivisions and industrial parks. Still, in most agricultural communities, the irrigation systems remain dynamic components of the local economies. The CCC improvements of the 1930s and early 1940s continue to serve farmers well.

7

Developing National Wildlife Refuges

The Fish and Wildlife Service Program

The U.S. Fish and Wildlife Service administered an important CCC program in terms of its contribution to Nevada's national wildlife refuges (NWRs). Following years of inadequate support, federal funds and free CCC labor became available at a critical time in wildlife-management history. The 1920s and early 1930s were troubling times for the Fish and Wildlife Service's predecessor agencies: the Bureau of Fisheries and the Biological Survey. While responsible for the conservation and protection of fish, wildlife, and plant habitats, the agencies lacked the resources to do the job right. Even after receiving permission to acquire land for refuge development, the passage of a bill to establish national refuge systems was a tough sell. After four rejections in eight years, the Migratory Bird Conservation Act was finally enacted into law in 1929. Despite modest strides, congressional appropriations were inadequate. The fledgling programs struggled until an advisory committee appointed by President Roosevelt drew attention to rampant habitat destruction caused by overharvesting and pervading droughts.[1] Public sentiment began to change under the Roosevelt regime.

With newly acquired refuge lands, the Department of Agriculture's Bureau of Fisheries and Biological Survey were restructured in 1939; consequently, the new Fish and Wildlife Service emerged under the purview of the Department of the Interior. The Fish and Wildlife Service and its predecessors utilized the CCC to construct of numerous refuge headquarters and wildlife habitats. In Nevada, three national refuges reaped benefits from the relief program: the Ruby Valley National Wildlife Refuge, Charles Sheldon National Wildlife Refuge, and Desert National Wildlife Range (DNWR).

In commemoration of the fifth anniversary of the CCC in 1938, Dr. Ira N. Gabrielson, chief of the Biological Survey, shared his optimism for the future of the national wildlife program: "Five years ago when our wild life resources, especially waterfowl, were in serious danger the biological survey had a restoration program. . . . Then emergency funds for buying refuge areas became available and the CCC help for developing them. The results being accomplished are laying the foundation for [a] wildlife restoration program beyond our fondest dreams."[2]

Gabrielson was confident that enrollees would gain from this unique learning experience. Young men were given "an opportunity to work with nature, watch how nature responds to those who work with it. City boys who never before saw ducks, geese, heron, egrets, sandhill crane, pheasants and other of our wild life have through the CCC . . . an opportunity to watch them thru their mating and nesting."[3]

Without question, enrollees who came from urban areas were exposed to the rugged beauty of nature like they had never known before. However, given their immaturity and limited life experience, the great outdoors did not always compensate for trips to the movies or dances in town. Furthermore, the remoteness and cold winters at Camps Ruby Lake and Sheldon were discomforting for the men, particularly those from the temperate South. To the dismay of camp personnel, low morale was a constant problem at Nevada's wildlife refuges.

Sheldon National Wildlife Refuge

The rugged location and extreme climate at the Sheldon National Wildlife Refuge also posed an acute problem for the army, which was responsible for running the camps and caring for the young men. The repercussions of building a permanent camp along the Nevada-Oregon border soon became evident. The first Bureau of Fisheries camp was constructed on a ranch known as Board Corrals, just west of the refuge boundary. The seasonal camp operated from mid-1935 until late 1937. With its ambitious agenda, the Biological Survey pushed for a year-round camp at Sheldon NWR. Still, the Ninth Corp Army headquarters was reluctant to build, maintain, and operate a permanent camp at this location. CCC inspector A. W. Stockman relayed the army's concerns in an eight-page letter to Assistant CCC Director J. J. McEntee:

> The area between the railhead [Winnemucca] and the area where the camp is situated is practically uninhabited and truck[s] en route to and from the railhead [that] might develop mechanical trouble or be involved in an accident would find the personnel many miles from any possible assistance. . . . Milk could be transported by refrigerator truck but it is believed that due to the nature of the roads

Enrollees cool off in a swimming hole at Camp Board Corrals, July 1937. Courtesy U.S. Fish and Wildlife Service

> that such milk upon arrival at camp would be in a separated condition and unfit for drinking purposes. . . . Denio, Oregon, which is approximately 35 miles from the camp site is a ghost town with only approximately 15 inhabitants. . . . [S]urgery or hospitalization in an emergency would be extremely hazardous as the nearest hospital facilities are at Winnemucca, Nevada, 138 miles distant over very rough roads. . . . In winter the temperature drops to 20 to 25 degrees below zero.[4]

The Biological Survey persevered and eventually won approval for the new camp after promising to shorten and improve the road between the camp and Winnemucca and provide extra recreation facilities for the isolated camp. According to a camp inspection report dated November 19, 1940, the federal agency lived up to its promise to construct a splendid sixty-by–one hundred–foot gymnasium. However, once logistical issues were resolved, new ones arose. It seemed that enrollees rarely used the facility and complained bitterly about the lack of heat. During biweekly movies, enrollees were forced to wear overcoats and blankets, and water buckets were frozen solid every morning. After investigating the complaints, the camp inspector reported that the "cold camp" was the fault of a controlling and insensitive camp commander. When the camp commander was asked why there were no stoves, he replied that they were there when he arrived, but he had not gotten around to setting them up. According to the inspector, "I never visited a camp where the enrollees, Adm. Personnel, Technical Personnel, Overhead, etal, [*sic*] were at such odds."[5]

The camp commander's dismissal offered some relief, although the underlying discontent lingered. The practicality of operating a year-round facility at Sheldon NWR continued to cause dissension among officials. Some questioned the army's decision to send southern men from the Fourth Corps Area to Camp Sheldon. Even the CCC camp inspector spoke up: "Personally, I believe that Dakato [*sic*], Montana or Wyoming enrollees . . . should have been sent to the camp."[6] The Biological Survey continued to make extra concessions to keep the camp open. To ensure a steady inflow of supplies during bad weather, emergency shelters equipped with stoves and fuel were constructed along the truck route between Winnemucca and Camp Sheldon.

Once added safety measures were in place, the Biological Survey was finally able to improve and develop the expansive, six hundred thousand–acre refuge.[7] Early CCC crews from the Board Corrals camp had concentrated their efforts on the west side of the refuge. From 1935 to 1937, the men constructed a rock-abutted road (State Route 34A) up the mountain to the west entrance of the refuge. The new road, with its 10 percent grade, was a major improvement over the former unreliable route with its 28 percent slope. They also built a more direct road from the Tom Dufurrena Ranch to the refuge headquarters. The Board Corrals crews are further credited with installing 102 miles of telephone line, including a connection to Cedarville, California, and constructing a number of small erosion-control, fencing, and spring-development projects.[8]

Camp Sheldon, established on the McGee Ranch in Virgin Valley, was the second CCC camp assigned to the Charles Sheldon NWR. A detail of men from Company 1915 with its large contingent of Nevada and Utah enrollees first occupied the camp in the summer of 1938. The company had just completed five years of improvements at the Hawthorne Naval Ammunition Depot.[9] In 1939, Camp Sheldon was officially made permanent. Company 5460 soon replaced Company 1915 and remained at Camp Sheldon until the end of the CCC program.

A somber Board Corrals kitchen crew prepared sandwiches for more than two hundred men each day, June 1937. Courtesy United States Fish and Wildlife Service

Overnight cabins were built for the convenience and safety of refuge personnel working in the far reaches of the refuge. The cabins at Sheldon National Wildlife Refuge were constructed of native rock to blend with the landscape, August 1937. Courtesy United States Fish and Wildlife Service

Most of Camp Sheldon's assignments were now on the east side of the refuge. One of their first tasks was to improve the outlet to the railhead in Winnemucca. This entailed building 55 miles of road between the refuge and Quinn River Crossing. Enrollees also constructed twenty-three dikes and dams in Virgin Valley, and converted the Dufurrena residence into a refuge manager's headquarters. The men were assigned another ambitious task: fencing the northern, southern, and western boundaries of the refuge.[10] To accommodate refuge employees, several outlying homesteads were restored, and overnight cabins were built for their use while on patrol.[11] Late improvements at the Virgin Valley Campground, including the stone bridge over the pool in the service yard and the bathhouse, are still used by campers.[12]

Ruby Lake National Wildlife Refuge

The Ruby Lake NWR was established near a significant waterfowl habitat along the Pacific and central flyways through northeastern Nevada. Establishing a year-round camp to build the refuge was as great a challenge as at the Charles Sheldon NWR. The six thousand–foot-high valley was miles from the nearest railhead, and practically inaccessible to the outside world. Not surprisingly, it took the Fish and Wildlife Service two years to open the Ruby Valley CCC camp, after achieving its NWR status in 1938. Progress at Camp Ruby Lake was continuously hampered by poor access and isolation.

Low enrollment and high enrollee turnover persisted throughout the life of the camp. By their own admission, camp commanders and superintendents underestimated the time and energy required to maintain good morale and to train the inexperienced workforce.[13] The high turnover rate was reported to national CCC officials in a camp inspection report: "Few remain more than one [six-month] period. This week-end . . . over one hundred and fifteen enrollees will leave for the 6th C.A. [Sixth Corps Area with headquarters in Chicago] for discharge. Principal reason, too isolated."[14]

Consequently, construction of the refuge headquarters and associated facilities was delayed due to understaffing. The CCC stayed the course and managed to implement an ambitious work plan, which included the building of new truck trails, headquarter buildings, dikes, and water-control structures. Despite a sluggish start, several projects were under way by the end of the first season. Skilled foremen were hired to train and mentor the inexperienced young men who required constant supervision. However, enrollees with work experience or with a strong desire to learn were soon trained as carpenters and found themselves building concrete forms, workbenches, and fences. Meanwhile, a group of less experienced men was temporarily detailed to southern Nevada to salvage buildings, grease racks, and supplies from closed Soil Conservation Service camps at Moapa (SCS-1) and Bunkerville (SCS-4). The salvaged materials were transported to a proposed campsite (FWS-4) at the Desert Game Refuge in southern Nevada.[15]

CCC "Quarterly Narrative Reports" describe the slow but steady progress made as enrollees were trained as carpenters, drivers, and heavy-equipment operators. The development of wildlife habitats and construction of headquarters were top priorities. Taking advantage of good weather, the CCC men forged ahead and constructed the refuge manager's residence, a service building with a basement for office space and truck storage, water-control structures, and canals and dikes for the wildlife habitat.

Enrollees learned to operate heavy equipment, such as a Cleat Track and the twelve-yard Le Tourneau scraper, to clear scrub and grade roadways into the refuge. Enrollees were also trained on the Osgood Dragline, which was used to build jetties and excavate canals though the Ruby Marsh. During August and September 1940 alone, eighteen thousand cubic feet of earth

Isolated Camp Ruby Lake was seventy-six miles from the nearest railhead at Wells. Courtesy U.S. Fish and Wildlife Service

was moved.[16] Refuge work was challenging, and the young men were anxious to complete training courses in order to earn the privilege of operating motorized equipment. For many enrollees, learning to operate a truck or tractor compensated for the lack of social amenities in Ruby Valley. Many of the men had never sat behind the wheel of a car, let alone drive earth-moving equipment. By the fall of 1940, Camp Ruby was suitably equipped with fifteen truck drivers, five backup drivers, and several heavy-equipment operators.

Beyond the refuge boundaries, enrollees helped establish communications between Ruby Lake NWR and the outside world. A crew of 12–18 enrollees from the nearby Division of Grazing's Camp Warm Creek (DG-82) assisted Ruby Valley enrollees with the telephone-line project.[17] The two camps completed 12 of 40 miles of new telephone line between the refuge and the Elko County Fish Hatchery, and another line between the Gardner Ranch in Ruby Valley and Murphy Ranch in Secret Valley.

Maintaining the momentum was difficult. Company strength fell to an all-time low in August 1941 when Company 5724 moved on. Their replacement was Company 2557 from the Desert National Wildlife Range.[18] A maximum strength of 156 men was reported in November 1941. A "Quarterly Narrative Report" addressed Company 2557's youthfulness, which was consistent with national trends during the final CCC years. On an average, most of the enrollees were seventeen or eighteen years old with a lesser number of men over twenty years in age. Most of the enrollees lacked an eighth grade education, and their home lives were described as "very poor."[19]

The new company was immediately put to work building major truck trails. A reliable transportation corridor was needed between the refuge and the railhead at Wells. Using a combination of heavy equipment and manual labor, the CCC built the 26-mile long "East Service Road." In all, Ruby Lake enrollees graded 52 miles of road surface, including 19 miles of county road, between the refuge and the oiled highway (State Route 229) that led to Wells. Before the camp closed, a laborer-patrolman's dwelling (now Quarters no. 17) and a rock-rubble water-control structure at the head of Cave Creek were completed.[20]

Camp Ruby Lake enrollee Herman Haynes had little trouble adjusting to the rural character of the camp. Being mechanically inclined, Haynes was trained to drive a truck at the refuge after proving himself to the company commander.

Camp Ruby Lake equipment operators built the East Road in 1940 using an elevating grader and an RD-7 Caterpillar tractor. Courtesy U.S. Fish and Wildlife Service

---

Herman Haynes, Camp Ruby Lake

At the time that I went into the Civilian Conservation Corps, I was living here in St. Louis with my mother. . . . My father . . . left many, many years ago. Really, my grandmother took care of my brother and I. That's why I went into the three-Cs in 1940, because my mother wasn't doing too well.

. . . [T]hings were pretty rough around the St. Louis area. . . . Several of my friends that I bummed with . . . joined the three-Cs, and at the time they were pretty close to home. . . . I thought, "Well, I'll join. . . . Maybe I'll be in one of the camps with my friends," but things didn't work out that way, so I was definitely surprised about going to Wells, Nevada.

I guess I was about eighteen. I graduated from grade school in 1937 and went to high school for about a half-year. I didn't care much for that. So, then I went to a vocational school . . . and learned to be a machinist, but at that time jobs were kind of sparse. . . .

I went down there and signed up and took the oath. . . . [Approximately thirty of us] were sent down to Jefferson Barracks. That was the army post at that time—very active. We were getting close to war, World War II, because there were an awful lot of soldiers down there. . . .

One morning, why, a train backed in, and we loaded on and began our trip to Wells, Nevada. Actually, they didn't tell us where we were going until we got there. At that time, I couldn't tell my mother where I would be sent. We went through Salt Lake City. We went across the salt flats, and of course, Wells, Nevada, is just west of the salt flats. . . . It was about the middle of January 1940—*very* cold. . . . There were trucks waiting to transport us to the camp in Ruby Valley, which was approximately eighty-one miles from Wells over an old gravel road, and it was quite a bumpy ride. . . . [T]o me it was a primitive area.

These men were from . . . all over the country. . . . We had men from Arkansas and Oklahoma. We used to call them "Oakies" and "Arkies." It was very educational, as far as meeting these different people, talking to them, getting to know them, and learning about differences. . . . In the morning the trucks went out—dump trucks—and there was a gravel pit about three-quarters of a mile from camp. They gave us picks and shovels, and we went out there and picked at the gravel and then loaded the trucks. The trucks were used to upgrade the roads around the Ruby Lake area and also toward Wells, Nevada. The real project was for the Fish and Wildlife Service. We had a big dragline where they were cleaning around the edge . . . and enlarging the lake itself. . . .

There was one other project . . . which was to start putting in a phone line from the Indian reservation to Wells, Nevada. We dug the holes and put in these telephone poles. . . . The Fish and Wildlife lake project was OK, and the roads were improved, but the phone line was incomplete [when we left].

Our commanding officer was First Lieutenant Robert E. Meek. . . . They chose me to take a driver's test for the army truck, and he went along. We drove along the [dike] road on the lake there, and it was kind of eerie at first, but then I got used to it. His idea, which I learned from talking to some of the other drivers, was that he would try to distract you—to make you look someplace where you weren't supposed to instead of keeping your eyes on the road. I knew all about what was going to happen, and I passed the test. . . . So I got the job of driving the army truck to go into town, get supplies, and also to run the PX. . . . A captain took care of supplies and also the PX, so I was more or less working for the captain after that.

One of the . . . trips I made . . . with the captain, we had to go into Salt Lake City to do some official business. So, we drove . . . into Salt Lake City and went up to Fort Douglas. It was an army camp right in the middle of town.

At that time we had governors on those trucks, and they would only go about thirty-five miles an hour . . . so being mechanically inclined, why, I disconnected the governor. . . . One day we were going to Wells. It was a long trip . . . and we were going along slowly. It was a rough road, and there were lots of culverts that made dips in the road. I just put the old pedal to the metal, and we were up to about sixty miles an hour. And that really surprised the captain, because he said, "What did you do?"

I said, "Well, I think it would be better if we get there quicker because it's a long trip." After that he didn't say anything.

We had a ball field there and played softball with the Indians. There was a reservation nearby. . . . [W]e went hiking at different areas around the camp—up the mountain and around the lake. . . . I guess most of the fellows had a few drinks and gambled with what they had. . . . I couldn't do much of anything because of being the designated driver. . . . Near the camp there was . . . a general store. I think the Indians ran it. Sometimes, they had drinks and things like that, and I'd take some members up there in the evenings . . . for recreation.

One of the interesting things we did . . . it was the Fourth of July. So the company commander . . . wanted me to take a group of guys on a rec[reation] trip to down around Ely, Nevada, for a two-day jaunt. One of the members got a little drunk, and he started flirting with the sheriff's wife. I think that we had to get him out of jail the next day when we left.

About the middle of summer or early fall, the camp broke up—dissolved. That sure surprised us, by golly. I think maybe that project . . . was pretty well along, and maybe that's why we got transferred to another camp: they sent us to Heber City, Utah, south of Salt Lake City. . . . [W]e were on the outskirts of town, which was great. We had a theater, a shopping center, and all. That was almost like being home. I spent about six or nine months at Ruby Valley. . . . All together I was in the three-Cs two years. . . . [A]fter a while, I enjoyed the CCC, and if I had to do it over, I probably would.[21]

Desert National Wildlife Range

Established in 1936, the Desert National Wildlife Range was created to protect the shrinking herds of desert bighorn sheep whose population had dipped to a record low of three hundred by the 1930s.[22] The wildlife range is the largest in the country, subsuming 1.5 million acres of rugged mountain ranges and desert basins in the southern part of the state. The Fish and Wildlife Service purchased the old Corn Creek Spring Ranch in 1939 for this purpose. Compared to the permanent CCC programs at Ruby Lake and Sheldon NWRs, this FWS program was short-lived. CCC camp rosters show that Camp Corn Creek was officially occupied for a month and a half during the summer of 1941. A severe windstorm caused major damage to the camp, which may partially explain why Company 2557 was transferred to Ruby Lake. However, a year earlier, Senator Pittman had urged the secretary of interior to cut a Biological Survey camp in favor of retaining Camp Newlands and helping Fallon farmers. Camps were being eliminated nationwide due to a reduction in CCC appropriations.[23]

Despite its seemingly short duration, sufficient progress was made the previous year by a Camp Las Vegas (DG/G-122) spike camp. According to a Las Vegas newspaper, the Grazing Service and Biological Survey collaborated on several range projects in the Sheep Range.[24] Mandated by the Taylor Grazing Act, range improvements provided water for livestock as well as dwindling bighorn sheep populations. The spike camp built twenty-four miles of truck trails from the wildlife range headquarters at Corn Creek Ranch to the Hidden Forest, and another twenty-seven miles of truck trail from the headquarters to Mormon Wells. To impound rainfall from summer monsoons, two million-gallon capacity earthen reservoirs were constructed in White Sage Flats and Three Lakes Valley (currently within the boundaries of Nellis Air Force Test and Training Range).[25] The Grazing Service developed several mountain springs with underground storage tanks and troughs. Access to the range was important, and the CCC-built roads made the countryside more accessible to stockmen, wildlife staff, and outdoor enthusiasts.[26]

Although the majority of range improvements were completed by the Grazing Service, it is possible that the Fish and Wildlife Service's short stint at the Desert National Wildlife Range focused on the protection of big game.[27] The Fish and Wildlife Service had a history of collaborating with other entities such as the Grazing Service. Using CCC labor, and in collaboration with the Park or Grazing Service, one hundred thousand dollars was supposedly allocated for the expansion of winter feed areas in the Boulder Canyon and Overton areas and at various points along the lower Colorado River.[28] Similarly, the Fish and Wildlife Service collaborated with the Grazing Service on spring developments and wildlife enclosures farther north, near Mason Valley.[29] Most important, the CCC received accolades for their accomplishments on the public lands in southern Nevada. According to an editor for the *Las Vegas Age:*

> The prevailing opinion that CCC operations have in general been wasteful, inefficient and not well directed is disproven by an inspection of the work done by Las Vegas Camp CCC [Company] No. 122. . . . Las Vegas certainly owes a vote of thanks to State Supt. Tom Miller; Supt. Jameson and Vegas CCC No. 122, which we must admit, have done something really fine and constructive for Clark County.[30]

8

Building Playgrounds in the Desert

The National Park Service and the CCC

Nevada residents wished for more parks and outdoor recreation facilities long before New Deal monies made them a reality. Nevada officials were also keenly aware of the revenue that tourism would generate for the rural state. But major obstacles stood in the way. Serious plans to develop recreation facilities were hampered by inadequate roadways and a lack of service facilities. Modest strides were made with the expansion of the state highway system in the 1920s. Highway expansion continued into the late 1930s following a surge of federal aid. By 1940, most U.S. and Nevada highways were either oiled or paved, and small towns were accessible by way of improved secondary roads.

Nevada officials had the foresight to begin park planning a decade earlier. In 1925, the Nevada State Legislature appropriated monies for a Nevada Transcontinental Exposition to celebrate the completion of the Lincoln Highway through Reno.[1] The legislature also took steps to exchange state property for more desirable federal lands. The first parcels exchanged were Fort Churchill in Churchill County followed by Kershaw Canyon (now Kershaw-Ryan State Park) in Lincoln County. In 1931, Congress authorized land acquisitions at Valley of Fire and Beaver Dam.[2]

As governor, James Scrugham was instrumental in drawing attention to Nevada's cultural and natural resources and strongly encouraged park development. Although the wheels were already in motion, FDR's New Deal programs spurred the massive expansion of parks and recreation facilities.[3] Two New Deal programs, the Public Works Administration and the Emergency Conservation Work (or the Civilian Conservation Corps) contributed significantly to the national movement. Appropriately, the National Park Service (NPS) assumed the role of steward and leader for nationwide recreation planning. The actual work programs, however, were developed by state park officials and superintendents. In their expanded role, the NPS provided state park systems with standardized guidelines and technical expertise. NPS guidance for the CCC projects was administered from their West Coast headquarters in San Francisco.[4] Decisive issues were handled by officials at the park service's Washington office and the national CCC director who collectively approved new state park projects, funding requests, and the placement of new camps.

At the request of the Department of the Interior, the State Park Commission was established in 1935 to assume jurisdiction over several new state parks in southern Nevada: Valley of Fire, Cathedral Gorge, Beaver Dam, and Kershaw Canyon (Kershaw-Ryan). Governor Richard Kirman appointed Thomas Woodnut Miller as chairman of the commission. Miller had been appointed superintendent of emergency conservation work at the Boulder Dam State Park in 1933 (CCC Camp SP-1); in 1936 he was promoted to the position of improvement supervisor in charge of Division of Grazing camps in Nevada and eastern California.[5] While a member of Congress, Scrugham gained approval for seven National Park Service camps in Boulder City, Overton, Panaca, and Weeks (Fort Churchill).

Camp Overton superintendent Thomas Woodnut Miller poses at the entrance to Boulder Dam State Park in 1934. Miller was later appointed improvement supervisor of Department of Grazing CCC camps in Nevada and northern California and served as a state park commissioner for many years. Courtesy Special Collections, University of Nevada, Reno Library

The most ambitious park developments occurred in southern Nevada, in part as a result of Hoover Dam (then Boulder Dam), completed in 1935. Nationwide interest was heightened by the largest federal project in the country and the creation of Lake Mead, the world's largest artificial lake of that era. Although the dam was primarily built to generate power and control downstream floods, the awe-inspiring structure and new lake became instant tourist attractions. According to Secretary of Interior Harold Ickes's estimate, a recreational area in this mild climate would eventually attract 500,000 or more visitors annually. Ickes was correct—in 1935 alone, 365,000 persons visited the dam and lake.[6]

To accommodate the influx of tourists, new park facilities were in demand. With CCC labor, the NPS developed beaches and outdoor facilities in three different areas of the Boulder Dam Recreational Area (later subsumed by Lake Mead National Recreation Area): Hemenway Wash near Boulder City, Overton Beach, and Pierce Ferry in Arizona.[7] The park service's CCC program accomplished its goals. NPS director Arno Cammerer was pleased with the "fine cooperation from the Civilian Conservation Corps."[8]

Enrollees and staff from the Boulder City and Overton camps provided the main labor force for the new recreation area. In addition to building new campgrounds, other ancillary tasks needed their attention. For example, grading and sanding the bathing beach (now Boulder Beach) in Hemenway Wash was greatly appreciated by local residents. To transform the stony slope into suitable beach, a half-mile-by–seven hundred–foot swath (on each side of the highway) was graded, leveled, and sanded.[9] The CCC built bathhouses and floating boat and swimming docks and created a desert oasis by planting lawns and trees in the new campground.[10] Boulder City enrollees also built the natural rock wall at the Lake Mead Overlook, a few miles west of the dam, so visitors could enjoy a breathtaking view of the new lake. When a skilled stonemason was laid off after building the first fifty feet of rock wall, enrollees completed the project. According to the park service superintendent: "The rock guardrail is a sturdy looking piece of work and is pleasing in appearance. . . . [E]nrollees were taught by the landscape architect (thru the foreman) to lay up the stone, and a good section of rock wall has resulted. It is surprising how quickly the boys caught on. . . . It is a sample of how much good work can be accomplished by a little patient instruction."[11]

Camp Boulder City (NP/SP-6) was apparently the first CCC program in

Camp Boulder City men constructing the rock wall at Lake Mead Overlook, west of Hoover Dam in 1936. Courtesy UNLV Library, Special Collections

Nevada to organize a volunteer fire department. Six Companies, Inc., the prime contractor at Hoover Dam, donated a small firehouse and fire truck for the protection of the CCC camp. However, that protection extended beyond the camps, and CCC men and volunteers also responded to fire calls in Boulder City. The CCC fire department had the support of the park service superintendent: "There is only a volunteer fire organization at Boulder City; the organization of a fire department of enrollees is a fine thing, we believe."[12]

To accommodate the dramatic increase in motorists, the highway between Las Vegas and Kingman, Arizona, was kept open year-round by 1936. Visitors came to southern Nevada by car, rail, and plane. The CCC helped extend and surface new runways at Bullock's Field in Boulder City. For several years, the Grand Canyon Airlines and Trans World Airlines scheduled regular stops in Boulder City for its planes on the Newark, New Jersey, and Los Angeles, California, route.[13]

Hoover Dam and Lake Mead immediately lured tens of thousands of tourists to southern Nevada. Grand Canyon Airlines and Trans World Airlines (TWA) added Boulder City to their scheduled stops. Residents and dignitaries celebrated TWA's inaugural flight on April 3, 1938. Courtesy McBride Collection, Boulder City/ Hoover Dam Museum

The Boulder City and Overton camps are probably best known for their involvement in salvage archaeology, most notably excavations at Lost City in the lower Moapa Valley. The rising Lake Mead threatened a number of important archaeological sites along the terraces overlooking the Muddy River. One well-publicized project was at Lost City, a five-mile stretch of Puebloan settlements that were soon to be inundated by Lake Mead.[14] In a race against time, Nevada and NPS officials mobilized the young and energetic labor force and resumed the excavation at Lost City.

Archaeological excavations at the large site had begun a decade earlier at the suggestion of Governor Scrugham, who was extremely interested in the ancient settlement and the attention that it brought to his state. The governor asked local residents John Perkins and Fay Perkins to research the early settlements. Fascinated by their initial findings, Scrugham solicited the help of archaeologist Mark Harrington from the Museum of the American Indian, Heye Foundation, in New York. At the time, Harrington was working at nearby Gypsum Cave. Data from Lost City (coined Pueblo Grande de Nevada by Harrington) forced archaeologists to reconsider the western extent of Puebloan cultures, once believed to be east of the Colorado River. After the 1924–1926 excavations drew to a close, the abandoned settlements fell victim to neglect and vandalism.[15]

Several years later, Harrington, then director of the Southwest Museum, accepted the park service's invitation to conduct salvage excavations at Lost City. In 1934 and 1935, Harrington and thirty-two enrollees and two foremen from Camp Overton excavated 5 pueblos, 16 pit dwellings of Basket Maker III age, and 5 early pit dwellings. By the close of 1936, their accomplishments included a total of 121 "ruins," including 610 rooms. For public education and artifact storage, the CCC constructed the Boulder Dam State Park Museum (now Lost City Museum) on a mesa south of Overton. The CCC also built a Basket Maker–period pit dwelling and an adobe and stone reconstruction of a Lost City pueblo on the museum grounds. Several other archaeological projects were conducted nearby. Harrington hired Fay Perkins and Willis Evans to supervise the Boulder City CCC boys on excavations at a prehistoric turquoise mine near the dam, at Willow Beach, south of Hoover Dam, and at Pierce Ferry at the lower end of the Grand Canyon.[16] Perkins also directed archaeological excavations at the new Valley of Fire State Park. Overton enrollee Charles Guy worked at the Valley of Fire and shared his impressions of fieldwork:

> I was on an archeological crew, going out . . . and digging. We'd go out there in the middle of no place—there was no roads out there then, you just drove across the desert. . . . One day I found half of an Indian bead. Just half of it. And you know we shoveled sand all day long lookin' for the other half of that bead and never did find it. . . . We found a lot of arrowheads. The arrowheads were the most popular things we found, the most plentiful. . . . Most of 'em weren't in perfect shape, would have the point broke off. . . . [Fay Perkins] was the easiest guy. All he wanted you to do was do your work.[17]

The CCC built a number of tourist and campground facilities and trails at the new Valley of Fire State Park. They built stone visitor cabins, ramadas

Camp Overton men hold ceramic pots—called "ollas"—recovered from Lost City excavations, ca. 1934. Courtesy NPS, Lake Mead National Recreation Area Archives

for shade, and roads into natural points of interest at the Valley of Fire. From parking areas, several trail systems leading to the blazing red-rock formations and petroglyph sites were also constructed.

Lincoln County was not far behind Clark County sites in terms of federal funds spent on park developments. The county received approval for a fair share of state-operated recreational facilities thanks to the collective efforts of the county commission, the Caliente Chamber of Commerce, state senator L. L. Burt, and Congressman Scrugham. Lincoln County was anxious to promote its little-known natural attractions, including the intense red spires and erosional features at Cathedral Gorge. After purchasing park properties with federal Public Works appropriations funds, Congressman Scrugham and Senator McCarran secured a CCC camp for Panaca to build new parks. A full company from Camp Overton was transferred to Panaca from the Lake Mead area to work at Cathedral Gorge, Kershaw Canyon, and Beaver Dam. The camp also worked on long-needed drainage and flood-control projects.[18]

Before the Lincoln County parks could be built, however, better access roads and a reliable source of water were needed. At Cathedral Gorge, a windmill encased in a forty-foot rock tower was built over an existing well sunk years earlier by local ranchers. For safety reasons, access roads leading from the Pioche-Caliente Highway (U.S. Highway 93) required straightening and resurfacing. Lincoln County obtained funds from the state highway

Men from Camp Overton excavating portions of the Willow Beach site south of Hoover Dam. Photo taken in October 1936. Courtesy National Park Service, Lake Mead National Recreation Area Archives

The CCC built this campground and stone tourist cabins (in background) at the Valley of Fire State Park in 1934. Courtesy U.S. Park Service Collection, University of Nevada, Las Vegas Library

system to improve roads from the Panaca Highway (State Route 317) to the Kershaw-Ryan State Park. The CCC redesigned existing roads and built new roads, parking areas, fire pits, and trails. Beaver Dam was quite a distance from the Panaca camp, so a spike camp with fifty enrollees was established on-site. Another spike camp was established at Lehman Caves National Monument, 145 miles to the north, after the U.S. Forest Service transferred the park to the National Park Service. The spike camp was tasked with improving the recreational facilities at the limestone cave and surrounding attractions.[19] Nevada wasted no time in promoting its new recreation and park facilities. The attractions were featured in Chamber of Commerce pamphlets, newspapers and magazines, and *The WPA Guide to 1930s Nevada,* published in 1940.[20]

Farther north, the park service was immersed in the restoration of Fort Churchill, an 1860s army post built along the Overland Emigrant Trail. Strategically located 65 miles east of Carson City, the post was abandoned in 1869 when its usefulness had passed. Soon thereafter, the fort began to crumble. On behalf of the Daughters of the American Revolution (DAR), Senator McCarran and Congressman Scrugham secured a CCC camp to restore the historic site. During the summer and fall of 1935, Camp Fort Churchill constructed a campground and a day-use area and built a number of park buildings. Pleased with the restoration and new facilities, the DAR presented the CCC with an American flag in a formal ceremony in June 1935.[21]

The Fort Churchill Project was unique in that it represented the first historic restoration in the state. The park service employed the most competent historical technician available in that vicinity to direct the restoration.[22] The restoration work was performed by Company 590 from northern California and the Midwest. Before work could begin, the CCC had to manufacture tons of adobe bricks. Making the bricks was a multistage process: the adobe was soaked overnight and placed in a horse-powered pug mill where it was mixed with sand and water. The mixture was poured into handmade molds that produced four bricks at a time. This process went on for days, as tens of thousands of bricks were needed. The making of adobe brick was complicated, and losses were heavy. Bricks made from an incorrect mixture of clay, sand, and straw frequently broke while drying or during handling. Elsewhere, the CCC made three to four times more brick than needed to account for breakage during the reconstruction of Mission La Purisima in Lompoc, California.[23]

Fort Churchill was one of two known Nevada camps to be assigned a camp artist (R. Reaver sketched work scenes at the Wells Siding–Bowman Reservoir Project near Logandale). Elwood Decker, a thirty-one-year-old café artist and muralist from California, captured the various steps of restoration, from brick making to the rebuilding of walls at the fort. Decker kept copious notes on the restoration project and, on occasion, the attitudes of his fellow enrollees: "I've found lots to draw and early in the morning it's wonderful. I can't understand why everybody doesn't like it. We are so close to Mother Earth."[24]

Months later, Decker's request for a transfer to a CCC program in the San Francisco–Berkeley area underscored prevalent racial segregation poli-

Camp artist Elwood Decker documented daily scenes of the CCC while engaged in the restoration of Fort Churchill in 1935. This drawing shows hundreds of sun-dried adobe bricks being loaded onto a flatbed truck. Thousands of bricks were manufactured on-site before the restoration could begin. Courtesy Nevada Historical Society

cies that pervaded the federal government at that time. His initial intrigue with the wide-open spaces did not make up for the lack of artistic and cultural amenities. Superintendent of the Treasury Department's Painting and Sculpture Section Edward B. Rowan supported Decker's request to be transferred to Camp San Pablo. CCC officials in Washington, D.C., later denied the request after learning that Camp San Pablo was reserved for black enrollees. Meanwhile, Decker's company was transferred to Berkeley, and thus the issue became a moot point. Decker maintained that he would have willingly joined the African American camp, citing an unprecedented national interest in "Negro" sculpture and his support of equal opportunity for all.[25] Although Decker sought more creative outlets for his talent, he left behind an invaluable representational record of the New Deal in progress at Fort Churchill.

Following the restoration of Fort Churchill, a Division of Grazing camp, DG-67, reoccupied the camp in 1937 and 1938. The DAR held Fort Churchill in trust until 1957 when it was officially declared a state park. Fort Churchill eventually achieved National Historic Landmark status in 1961. In recent years, displays have been added to the Fort Churchill and Lost City Museums to commemorate the CCC contributions at the park. Over the years, scores of former enrollees have returned to Fort Churchill while vacationing out West.

Raymond Fry, Camp Fort Churchill (NP/SP-5)

I was from Missouri. I come almost to staying out there. . . . The wages were a little better out West. . . . We farmed. There was eight of us children. That was a big family.

[After joining the CCC] we went to Fort Leavenworth and made up a whole trainload, and we went to Los Angeles and up the coast to Vacaville. . . . I was twenty-one. A lot of them weren't but seventeen or eighteen and up.

We left Vacaville and went to Meeks Bay [Lake Tahoe] . . . and worked some . . . in a park, and in a few weeks they sent forty of us over to Fort Churchill and called it a spike camp. . . . We had small tents there. We worked there that summer, and in the fall they sent us back to the main camp at Meeks Bay. . . .

We made brick and tried to build [the fort] up. We tried different mixtures of sand and clay, and we finally thought we had pretty good brick, but I think some of them crumbled down last year when I was back there.

They dug clay out of one place, and we mixed them. We had a horse rented that turned the thing [pug mill] to mix the brick. We molded them out on the ground, and then covered them with sand and let them dry for a few weeks, and then they went to pick them up.

After Meeks Bay . . . we moved over to Berkeley, Wild Cat Canyon. I built trails and roads and even worked on a golf course down there in Oakland.

And I quit and came home in 1937 in March, back to Missouri. . . . I got homesick, I guess. . . . I'm getting plenty old now. I'm eighty-seven [in 2000], but my sons, they take me back . . . about three times. It had been about fifteen years since I'd been there [Fort Churchill] when we went last year.[26]

Search and Rescue

As with other CCC programs, park service enrollees performed an invaluable search-and-rescue function. One well-publicized tragedy occurred during the winter of 1936–1937. Boulder City enrollees from Camp NP/SP-4 spent several days trying to rescue the storm-marooned Prettyman party from near the Nevada-Maryland Mine in the Groom Range (northwest of Las Vegas). The rescue team included the sheriff and several park service staff. The group managed to save four individuals, although one person died while NPS Caterpillars attempted to reach him. The harrowing drama was front-page news for several days. The rescuers' diligence did not go unnoticed. Thanks to mine owner Lee Prettyman, Captain Charles Hall and 150 enrollees were officially acknowledged by President Roosevelt in a letter sent through CCC director Robert Fechner's office.[27]

Despite the tremendous strides made in the 1930s, the Nevada Park Commission lost momentum with the onset of World War II. Funds were diverted to the war effort, and parks suffered from neglect and limited maintenance. The situation would not improve until the commission was reorganized in 1953.[28]

9

Military Expansion in Hawthorne

The Navy and the CCC

A tragic accident at Lake Denmark, New Jersey, in 1926 helped to seal Nevada's future as a major military hub. The explosion at the U.S. Navy's ammunition depot totally destroyed the facility and wreaked havoc in the nearby community. Twenty-one people lost their lives, and scores more were injured in the mishap.[1] A thorough investigation stated the obvious for the sake of safety, munitions needed to be stored in a rural, less populated area.

After scouting locations in northern Nevada and eastern California, the navy selected Hawthorne as the site for a new ammunition depot.[2] On October 27, 1926, President Calvin Coolidge signed Executive Order no. 4531 withdrawing approximately 325 square miles of public domain immediately north of Hawthorne for use as a naval reservation. Almost overnight, the quiet railroad town of Hawthorne was transformed into a lively military town. Nine years later, in 1935, President Roosevelt expanded the reserve's boundary to include Cottonwood and Corey Canyons and the upper part of Baldwin and Lapon Canyons along the eastern slopes of the Sierra Nevada.[3]

By September 1930, the core construction of the Naval Ammunition Depot (NAD) was complete. For safety purposes, the depot's location in Hawthorne was ideal, although a shortage of water was a major constraint to the facility's future growth. This realization was heightened following a 1934 drought that depleted the depot's water reserves. The drought demonstrated that the watersheds high in the Sierra Nevada could not provide sufficient water to meet the navy's needs. Drought-related problems did not stop there. Mount Grant's overgrazed and sparsely vegetated slopes suffered serious erosion following a series of cloudbursts.[4] Depot officers, in collaboration with the U.S. Forest Service, agreed that additional watersheds must be tapped, impounded, and diverted to the depot. To combat hillside erosion, gullies and drainages had to be stabilized and revegetated.

However, in order to implement their plans, the navy would have to build roads to the upper-elevation watersheds.

The Hawthorne community and the navy lobbied to receive a CCC camp and solicited the help of their national representatives in Washington, D.C. Congressman Scrugham promised to "exert every effort in this behalf."[5] Although the navy would directly benefit from a CCC program, townspeople also looked forward to the economic stimulus that this New Deal program would bring. Meanwhile, U.S. Navy Inspector of Ordnance Capt. H. S. Babbitt compiled a wish list of projects to be completed by the CCC.[6] New roads to the summit of Mount Grant and into Cottonwood Canyon were priorities. The CCC would also build a new landing field and rifle range, rebuild earthen mounds on magazines and reinforce barricades, contour and reforest the Cat Creek watershed, and construct a dam in Rose Creek Meadow.

The community was successful in its bid for a CCC program. Hawthorne was granted its first CCC camp late in 1933, followed by a second camp in 1935. Local men from Hawthorne and Mina were immediately hired to build the first camp within the boundaries of the naval depot; the second camp was later constructed immediately south of the initial camp. Camp N-2 was initially manned by a company from New York and New Jersey.[7]

Scores of Nevada boys were recruited for the Hawthorne camps, and others were transferred from Camp Moapa. Of all the Nevada camps, Hawthorne, and Lamoille and Berry Creek in northeastern Nevada, employed the highest percentage of Nevada residents. To illustrate, Nevada's entire quota of eighty-eight men was assigned to Camp Hawthorne for the eighth enrollment period (October 1, 1936, through March 31, 1937).[8]

Several projects at the depot were performed in collaboration with other relief programs, including the WPA. Neither was it unusual for enrollees to work alongside men from the newly established transient camp on the Lucky Boy Mining Company property in Cottonwood Canyon. The facility was one of several established statewide to relieve small communities from the burden of caring for a growing transient population. At one point, about half of the two hundred men at the Cottonwood Canyon transient camp worked at the naval depot. In fact, those individuals who met the age and fitness criteria were allowed to join the CCC when openings occurred.[9]

The navy's CCC program was closely monitored by Nevada's elected officials. Not surprisingly, Captain Babbitt established a close friendship with Senator Pat McCarran while lobbying for CCC assistance. Once his projects were under way, Captain Babbitt wrote to the senator and invited him on a trip to the top of Mount Grant:

> Senator McCarran: If you have a chance, I would like very much for you to stop over here with me, one night at least, sometime this summer, and make a day's trip with me (it will take nearly all day) . . . to Rose Creek Reservoir; up Cottonwood Canyon to Grant Peak (11,200 feet elevation, all over a good graded road); then down via Big Indian and Corey Canyon Road. This is a trip you cannot duplicate in the Sierras, nor in Death Valley. It cannot be excelled, as to scenery & vistas. And you can look over my mineral collection (I have a pretty good one).[10]

From the beginning, Senator McCarran gave his unconditional support for the developments at the naval depot. The senator's distaste for obstacles, including Babbitt's pending retirement, is easily surmised from a handwritten note to a staff member:

> Please write Mr. Fechner (sign my name) urging the retention of these two E.C.W. camps at the Hawthorne Munitions Depot. They have done and will continue most necessary and important work. Write a letter to the Sec[retary] of the navy urging that Capt. Babbitt be retained and not retired until he completes the ECW program at the Depot. Don't say that Babbitt has suggested it. I am doing this on my own accord because I heard Babbitt was up for retirement. Don't send any copies to Babbitt—Send this carbon on to me. These military matters must be handled with gloves.[11]

When Babbitt retired in May 1937, he was sorely missed.[12] Nonetheless, work at the depot continued in earnest. By early 1936, CCC crews had completed the construction of 45 miles of mountain roads leading to watersheds in Corey and Cottonwood Canyons. The Cottonwood Canyon Road, which ascends 11,000 feet in elevation over the summit of Mount Grant, was a formidable achievement in its own right. At the time, only two other roads in the United States extended to similar or higher elevations—one of which traversed Pike's Peak in the Colorado Rockies.[13] The new roads also facilitated fire prevention and aided military horse patrols in charge of depot security. To protect the new roads and prevent eroded hillsides, the CCC tackled reforestation and afforestation projects along gullies and watersheds in "North Cat, Middle Cat, South Cat, Upper Cottonwood, and Upper Cory [Canyons]."[14]

One of the CCC's most important contributions was the well-engineered twenty-six-million-gallon capacity reservoir and dam in Rose Creek Meadow.[15] The Rose Creek Reservoir was an incredible undertaking due to its location more than halfway up the mountainside. The labor-intensive water impoundment was largely constructed by manual labor and horse-drawn Fresno Scrapers. The long-term advantages of the Rose Creek Reservoir live on as the reservoir continues to provide a significant source of water to this day. Subsequent efforts focused on transporting additional water to the depot on the valley floor. CCC crews soon completed a 4.5-mile duplicate water-supply system (pipeline) and the 11,000-foot-long Squaw Creek supplementary line by tapping into the Rose Creek pipeline.

Camp Hawthorne was tasked with building several new roads up to Mount Grant watersheds, including this road to Squaw Creek (2001 photo). Photograph by Renée Corona Kolvet

---

Opposite, top. Enrollees pour concrete into wooden forms at Squaw Creek intake, 1935. From here, water was transported by pipeline to the Hawthorne Ammunition Depot. Courtesy McCarran Collection, Nevada Historical Society

Opposite, bottom. Camp Hawthorne men used horse-drawn Fresno Scrapers to excavate Rose Creek Reservoir halfway to the summit of Mount Grant in 1935. Courtesy McCarran Collection, Nevada Historical Society

The naval depot also completed several ancillary projects. By 1936, the CCC had installed eleven reserve fuel and oil tanks, rehabilitated (sanded and oiled) eighty-four weapon magazines; oiled fifteen miles of auxiliary roads through housing and industrial compounds, built a three-mile-long telephone line, and constructed a forty-six-acre emergency landing field.

Despite formidable progress, Captain Babbitt requested that CCC camp M-1 be continued through the ninth enrollment period (in October 1937).[16] One source of frustration was the unexpected work required to fix leaks in the Rose Creek Reservoir. To remedy the problem, huge quantities of fill dirt were hauled in from twenty miles away, and the surface of the inner basin was coated with bentonite.[17] Following costly repairs, the reservoir performed as planned.

Overall, Hawthorne residents welcomed the young men stationed at the CCC camps. After all, residents were accustomed to new faces long before the CCC arrived. Navy and marine troops from around the country had been stationed in Hawthorne since the late 1920s. In fact, the town witnessed a healthy growth rate as a result of the military presence. To illustrate, the sparsely populated Hawthorne precinct (including Babbitt) had 244 residents in 1920. By 1930 that number had increased threefold to 757. By 1940, the area's population reached 1,220, a 500 percent increase over a span of twenty years.[18] Population growth brought recognition to the sleepy little community. Military men and CCC enrollees patronized local businesses and participated in community activities. Several CCC boys actually finished their high school education at Hawthorne Public School. Service groups and fraternal organizations went the extra mile to welcome newcomers by sponsoring competitive sports, dances, and plays. Hawthorne's small-town hospitality helped to ease the men's loneliness.

Living conditions at Nevada's CCC camps were generally good, although problems with disgruntled enrollees occasionally attracted the quartermaster's attention. Logistical concerns and poor living conditions were at the root of most of the complaints. The recurrent lack of clothing and supplies was attributed to Camp Hawthorne's distance from the quartermaster's office in Sacramento. Deficiencies in the number of cots and bed linens were noted in a "Camp Inspection Report" for Camp M-1.[19] Action was quickly taken, and the order for bedding was filled; however, a new problem soon arose.

In July 1937, a "Camp Inspection Report" casually mentioned problems with bedbugs "from time to time," claiming that the vermin were "always promptly exterminated." However, the bedbug issue proved to be more serious than originally believed. CCC inspector M. J. Bowen reported that forty boys, mostly transients or drifters, were discharged as absent without leave (AWOL) over a three-month period.[20] However, a letter from the Department of Public Welfare in Provo, Utah, to the director of CCC selection in Salt Lake City revealed a very different situation:

> During the last C.C.C. enrollment, a number of boys were sent from the Provo Camp to the Camp [Company] No. 1915 at Hawthorne, Nevada under Captain H. E. Wentsch. Some of these boys were recently enrolled, but a good many of them were boys who had been in the camp some time and were within one to three months of having served sufficient time to be honorably discharged. It has now been reported to us from a number of authentic sources that there has been a rather wholesale desertion from the camp by these boys . . . [who] were among the best men and made some of the best records that have been made under Captain Sessions of the Provo Camp. These boys report that upon their arrival at the Nevada Camp they found the beds infested with bedbugs and other vermin. Some of them did not remain a single night. . . . I am writing this letter because I feel men . . . should not receive an administrative discharge for desertion if there is cause for such desertion. . . . I feel some investigation should be made with respect to this. . . . I wish to state further that there is considerable resentment on the part of the parents of these boys due to the conditions reported.[21]

Secretary of Labor W. Frank Persons forwarded the letter to the assistant CCC director, J. J. McEntee, within a month of the complaint. Interestingly, the *Mineral County Independent and Hawthorne News* failed to cover the enrollee walkouts. Suffice it to say that the desertions were untimely and occurred amid Congressman Scrugham's campaign to extend Camp Hawthorne, slated to close that fall. In fact, Inspector Bowen traveled to Hawthorne on July 14 to assess whether Camp M-1 should be retained or abandoned.[22] His ambiguous report on the desertions may be explained in one or two ways: either political pressure influenced his downplaying of events or he was not fully informed of the situation by the camp commander.

These internal problems proved to be insignificant in comparison to world events that would soon affect the depot. By now, there were strong indications that the United States would be joining its allies on the European war front. The depot's growing importance to the country may have influenced the decision to retain Camp Hawthorne for another year and a half. During this time, the CCC not only completed the Mount Grant water and road projects but also assisted with several unplanned endeavors. For example, following a washout in Del Monte Canyon, CCC men built several new sections of road between Hawthorne and Aurora and a section of the Bodie Road, within a half mile of the Nevada-California state line.[23]

The navy's program was suspended in July 1938 after FDR ordered the closing of all U.S. Army and Navy CCC camps. The remaining Hawthorne enrollees were transferred to other camps in Nevada and California. A Grazing Service camp (G-119) later reoccupied Camp Hawthorne. Company 3273 was mainly composed of men from New York and New Jersey. The men worked on spring developments in the Huntoon Valley area until May 1941.[24]

After the termination of the CCC program in 1942, the two Hawthorne camp facilities were merged and transformed into Camp Jumbo. This massive facility housed a few thousand civilian workers hired to construct additional magazines, enlarge depot facilities, and supply ordnance for World War II. This influx of civilian men far outnumbered the CCC enrollees. Nonetheless, the accomplishments of this new group of workers did not overshadow the earlier accomplishments of the CCC. Enrollee Marshall Crawford recalled his CCC days and the experience he gained while helping build the first roads up Mount Grant.

Marshall Crawford, Camp Hawthorne (M-1)

I think that some friends of mine told me about the CCCs. . . . I think maybe it was Mr. Barton . . . the . . . county assessor. . . . They had an office open in the courthouse. So I went down and signed up, and sure enough they accepted me. You didn't have to know anything to go to work for the three-Cs back then. . . . There were four more from Yerington that went to that particular three-C camp that I remember. One of them was Bruce Miles, and one of them was Darrell (we just called him Del) McIntire. There was William Newcomb and Jack Newcomb, two brothers.

I got there fairly early in the development of this one particular three-C camp [Camp Hawthorne]. It might have been in December 1933. . . . Anyway my first job was helping the painter. They had a painter who painted all the telephone poles and power poles that ran around the base with red and white striping. . . . So I lugged paint. It could have been worse, if I hadn't been used to working, but I had my first job when I was eleven, and I had to be on the job every day, so I knew what it was to work.

There was one guy that we called "The Can't-Take-It Kid." He was from Detroit. He'd say, "Oh! I just can't take it!" Well, he was as tough as everybody: he could take it. We all complained about things, but we had a lot of expressions—some of them weren't very polite things to say. . . . I don't think it was very hard on us. . . . I had worked an awful lot harder than that in the hay fields and shoveling coal. . . .

After we got all the poles around there painted, there wasn't anything for me to do except go to work on the igloos. Now, those igloos were storage buildings to store bombs in, and the navy would load them with a powder inside. . . . They were like a potato cellar. . . . They had heating and cooling units inside that kept them at a constant temperature. . . . They were partly underground and partly aboveground. . . . [T]hey covered them with sand. . . .

I got on that crew that replaced the sand on the igloos—hopefully, as fast as the wind blew the sand off. It had to be done by shovels and wheelbarrows. They'd dig a hole in the sand, forty or fifty feet away from the igloo. We had shovelers to shovel the wheelbarrow full of sand, and then, somebody had to wheel the thing full of sand to the top of the igloo and dump it. . . . [U]sually it ended up being me that had to spread the sand out, trying to get it in the regular depth of thickness. They looked like a quonset hut, except they were much longer and they were concrete. I worked on that for maybe two or three months.

When spring broke, they developed this program for building a truck trail. It went from the road that connects Schurz and Hawthorne, up a canyon called Cottonwood Canyon. There was a little bit of a trail there, a dirt road part of the way. I got on the survey crew, because I knew Bruce Miles from Yerington. He was a college man, and he was studying engineering. . . . That was the job I had the rest of the time that I spent in the three-Cs.

He would survey, and then he would put in stakes. I got to carry stakes by the hundreds and drive the stakes down there where they told me. Then in surveying the center line of the road, they used a fill-in line . . . actually, it was a transit—a telescope with crosshairs in it. Every hundred feet we put in a stake. I only carried about fifty stakes at a time—as many as I could get in my arms. . . .

Well, then I graduated to running the level rod. . . . We surveyed the road as it wound. . . . We had to make a lot of switchbacks . . . in order to get up to the top of the mountain. It was too steep to be driving up it. . . . Jack and Bill Newcomb were bulldozer operators. We had a grader: it was a motorized grader. We had a couple of shovel operators. That was the earth-moving equipment. . . . The road I worked on was just one of several roads that the three-Cs worked on.

At first . . . we were driving from the main camp . . . near Hawthorne, right next to the navy base. So then it got to be quite a distance, quite a trip, and took quite a while to move our men . . . so they started what they called a spike camp. We stayed in tents in the spike camp at the top of Cottonwood Canyon. . . . [W]e finally got over to right where Cottonwood Canyon ends and Lapon Meadows begins. . . . The spike camp was sort of up on the summit.

Lapon Meadows is an old place where, way back in the early days, they had a placer mine going. There was gold there, a little. They really tore it up getting the gold out. There were some interesting things about that area. I always used to like to go around, you know, kind of an amateur archaeologist. On Sundays, if we didn't go somewhere else, I would wander around the hills. There is a big grove of mountain mahogany up there that the deer frequented, and I found Indian artifacts in that grove. . . . There were lots of sage hens . . . you could walk right up to within ten feet of them . . . they had never seen people.

They hauled water up to us. Well, there was a creek there. . . . They also had water for showers: they had a lister bag, a big canvas sack that hangs from poles. . . . It had a spraying thing at the bottom. . . . Well, we didn't ever take too long a shower, but they were *big*.

They had an army captain there that ran the CCC camp, and his name was Livingood: we never saw him. Well, the man who ran the camp was a Mr. Billings, an engineer, and he was a fine man. He was the man who really did the business about the building. I never heard of anyone taking off or going AWOL. Life wasn't that tough. . . .

Whenever you've got 150 guys living . . . close together, you are going to have arguments. That's what they put up that ring for. You know, these guys that would get into a fight or an argument, why they'd go at it in the ring with gloves. That was a good thing, because it kept somebody from being hit over the head with a two-by-four.

Yes, there were altercations. . . . Some of these fellows from Utah were Mormon fellows, and they were pretty defensive, because some of these other guys were not Mormon, and sometimes they made some disparaging remarks about Mormons. . . . You just have to get along with other people, because we lived in this barrack, and we were in there every night, except when we were up at the spike camp. . . .

Generally speaking, I think it was a good thing. I figure it was a thing that was needed at the time. In prosperous times, I don't think we would need it very much. But those guys weren't even eating right before they got in the three-Cs. Our clothes weren't just exactly the kind that we liked to wear either. . . . But they gave us a fatigue cap—just like they had in the army in World War II . . . shirts, pants, underwear, shoes—we had all that. We had boots and they were good boots. When they gave me my boots, this was the first time in my life I ever had the proper fit. They had this thing and they measured feet. They said, "You wear an 8B."

I said, "I don't either. I wear a 7."

"No, you don't. You wear an 8B."

And they gave me the 8B, and boy, I didn't like that at all for the first couple of hours, and then they got *so comfortable.*

Young people usually have things that they need to learn. I was nineteen when I got out of the three-Cs . . . very shortly after we got to the top of Mount Grant, so as soon as that survey job was over. . . . One of the things that induced me to quit the three-Cs was—the rumor got out that they were going to bring in a whole bunch of army guys and give us military training, and I didn't like that idea at all. . . .

I talked to Mr. Billings when I told him I was going to leave. He was the man in charge. He must have been fifty years old, and talking to him he said: "Well, Marshall, if you would just get a pair of glasses and stay here, I'll make a civil engineer out of you in five years." . . .

I needed glasses when I went into the CCC, but I was too stubborn to get them and I was embarrassed about having to wear glasses. . . . So I learned that you should be careful that you don't get too impetuous about what you don't want to do—makes for a bad decision. Financially, I would have been a lot better off if I'd have done exactly what he said. Banking never paid anything.[25]

10

Building Ranger Stations and Mountain Parks

The National Forest Service's CCC Program

In recent years, the U.S. Forest Service has devoted considerable effort to documenting its historic structures and improvements on national and state forest lands. In fact, one study shows that 160 of the Humboldt-Toiyabe Forest's 300 buildings are now considered historic, that is, more than fifty years old.[1] One does not have to look far to find evidence of the contributions of the Civilian Conservation Corps. A 1948 report to district rangers on the Humboldt National Forest stated, "Most of our buildings were built by the CCCs."[2]

The Roosevelt administration is credited with "bankrolling" the purchase of additional forestland during the Great Depression years. In Nevada, many land acquisitions were made to conserve overgrazed forestlands and critical watersheds along the eastern Sierra Nevada and the Humboldt River and its tributaries.[3] Emergency conservation work provided employment to technically trained foresters (engineers, architects, mechanics, and woodsmen) who in turn directed CCC enrollees in scores of challenging projects in the forests.[4] Similar to the National Park Service, constructing recreational facilities was a New Deal priority in Forest Service circles. Promoting tourism and providing access to Nevada's backcountry was foremost in foresters' minds. Using CCC and WPA labor, ranger stations and related facilities sprang up in forests around the state. Within a few years, new recreational facilities, including campgrounds, hiking trails, and ski huts, were available for residents and visitors alike.

During the CCC era, Nevada National Forest (now Humboldt-Toiyabe National Forest) fell under the administration of Intermountain Region 4, with headquarters at Fort Douglas, Utah.[5] Nevada's seven Forest Service CCC camps were established in forests throughout the state. However, the Forest Service's most ambitious CCC project was in southern Nevada on Mount Charleston.

As elsewhere, Forest Service CCC crews were often assisted by civilians or WPA workers. Enrollees helped ranchers and townspeople wage war on Mormon crickets. While the Division of Grazing fought them on the public domain, the Forest Service fought the battle in forestlands. Year after year, the unwelcome pests made the news. An article in the *Eureka Sentinel* reported on an all-day skirmish near Carlin during the summer of 1936:

> The United States Department of Agriculture's war on northeastern Nevada's Mormon cricket horde reached a climax yesterday when the insects made an assault on the town of Carlin. Two crews of workers augmented by a large number of extra men sent from Elko, battled a moving mass of crickets on the outskirts of the railroad town for 14 hours and were not certain whether they or the crickets would win the fight. . . . [T]he crickets extend along a front from Carlin for seven miles back to Lynn Creek, and have a depth of about ten miles.[6]

The Forest Service's CCC program blazed new roads and trails into prospective campgrounds, existing mines, or susceptible fire zones. The Forest Service with its ample staff of engineers and natural resource specialists provided technical expertise for CCC projects. Similarly, the technical staff assisted the Soil Conservation Service by supervising construction activities on southern Nevada flood-control projects in the lower Moapa Valley, Panaca, and Caliente (see chapter 11).

Similarities in construction and design in different forests are no coincidence. Most early ranger stations, roads, and campgrounds were built according to standard regional plans prepared by architectural engineer George Nichols in Utah. After 1938, a manual with standard plans and modifications was compiled by officials in Washington, D.C.[7] Although rustic designs using logs were popular in forests across the nation, Nevada's ranger stations were usually simple wood-frame buildings with stone or concrete foundations. The exteriors were clad with drop siding and green wood trim. Today these buildings retain their original appearance, although the white buildings we see today were originally a sage-green color.[8]

Nevada's first Forest Service CCC camps were established in Lamoille Canyon and Berry Creek, both in northeastern Nevada, and at Kyle Canyon on Mount Charleston, near Las Vegas. Similar to Camp Hawthorne, the first Forest Service camps were predominantly filled with Nevada men. Of the 225 men at Camp Berry Creek, at least 200 were White Pine County residents.[9] Elsewhere, the original 36 men sent to build Camp Charleston Mountain were southern Nevadans.[10]

Enrollees assigned to early forest projects lived and worked in some of Nevada's finest locations. Company 973 stationed at Camp Lamoille was so pleased with their surroundings that they submitted an article to the CCC's national newspaper, *Happy Days:*

> We are situated in Lamoille Canyon, in the majestic Ruby Range. . . . We are proud of our scenery, which is not unlike that of the Alps. The main object of this camp is to open up this marvelous region by building a road into the heart of the mountains where there will be a park with picnic grounds, good fishing from lakes and creeks that are fed by perpetual snow, and a great variety of marvelous scenes to keep your Brownie or Graflex busy. . . . When climatic conditions prevent us from remaining here any longer we will take our bed and walk, no, we will ride to Paradise Valley where we will hibernate until further notice.[11]

Camp Lamoille maintained its excellent standing long after the arrival of Company 2512 in 1936. A "Camp Inspection Report" emphasized the "splendid morale, good cooks and bakers, capable officers and forestry personnel, well policed buildings and camp grounds."[12] Camp Lamoille was not alone in its glory. Camp Berry Creek, north of Ely, was named the best of twenty-five camps in the Fort Douglas District in 1933.[13] With its large composition of local men, the Camp Berry Creek's open house drew fifteen hundred friends and relatives, who, amid dancing and singing, managed to consume twenty-eight hundred buns and two hundred pounds of bread within two hours of arrival.[14] *Ely Daily Times* reporter Gus Newman toured the camp and several field projects while writing a story on Camp Berry Creek. Newman was pleased with the hearty food and the camaraderie of the men and was impressed by the construction in progress, including four buildings at the Berry Creek Ranger Station. The reporter reiterated a presidential message read to enrollees during their lunch break. The message stressed one fundamental tenet of CCC employment: "Lieut. Epps read a memorandum from President Roosevelt confirming the fact that the conservation camps will be renewed for a six month period, but urging each man to make an honest effort to secure a job before signing up again. 'But do not accept a job that will mean loss of work for another man.'"[15]

Within six months, the men of Camp Berry Creek developed new campgrounds in the Duck Creek area, and improved existing facilities at East Creek, Bird Creek, Berry Creek, and Steptoe Creek.[16] The men improved the recreational area at Lehman Caves by adding a public campground and parking areas and piping water to the park. Later, the National Park Service assumed administration of the caves.[17]

After closure of the camp, many men returned to part-time work at Nevada Consolidated Copper Company in McGill. Others returned to school or were transferred to a Soil Conservation Service CCC camp in Moapa Valley to work on flood-control projects.[18] Other Forest Service camps relied on workforces from the East Coast, Midwest, and later on the South. Company 1212 from New York spent the most time in Nevada forests and rotated between the Paradise and Lamoille camps from 1937 through mid-1940. Toward the middle of this stint, seventy-two men from Hackensack, New Jersey, replaced discharged New Yorkers.[19] A CCC *Pictorial Review* (yearbook) reflects Company 1212's first impression of Paradise Valley: "It was quite a change to be transferred from the metropolitan location near New York City to the silence of northwestern Nevada. Here the men were located in something of a ghost town, for this region was once more prosperous than at the present time."[20]

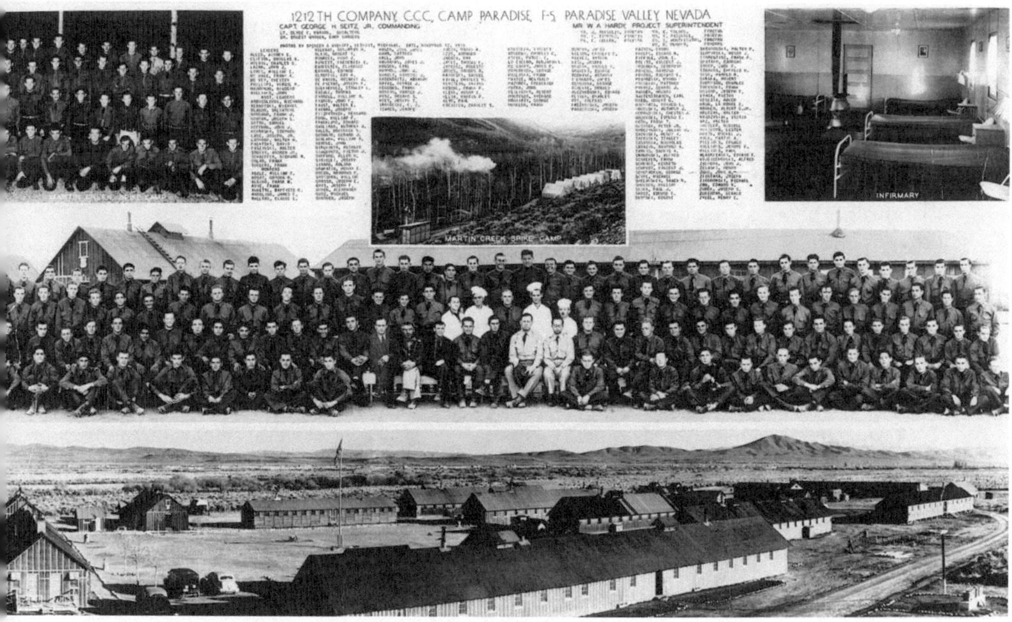

A group photograph was taken of Company 1212 from Camp Paradise on November 17, 1939. Courtesy Humboldt-Toiyabe National Forest

Work on the forests was often similar in nature to work performed by the Grazing Service on the open range. National Forest supervisor Alexander McQueen, George Larson's replacement, summarized the work planned for the eastern and central counties: "Roads, trails, range water developments, and administrative buildings will be maintained in all counties having national forest land. . . . Reposting of forest boundary will be a project in these counties."[21] With dynamite and heavy equipment, Camp Paradise crews widened and improved several roads, including a thirty-five-mile stretch over the eight thousand–foot Hinkey Summit that connected Paradise Valley with U.S. Route 95. The CCC work was impressive and aesthetically pleasing. For example, Camp Paradise stonemasons built more than one hundred rock-masonry bridges and abutments along Hinkey Summit. Enrollees also fenced the twenty-eight-mile perimeter of the forest reserve around their camp.[22]

Establishing communications between outlying ranger stations was imperative. Crews built roads and telephone lines between the Paradise Valley Ranger Station and the outlying station at Martin Creek.[23] The men also constructed the administrative buildings at Paradise Ranger Station and the forest supervisor's compound in Elko.[24] The construction of the Elko–Mountain Home road generated widespread interest and attracted dignitaries including Senator Pat McCarran, Governor Richard Kirman, Congressman James Scrugham, Attorney General Gray Mashburn, and state and highway officials.[25]

Nevada's seven Forest Service CCC camps were established in valleys, canyons, high mountain ranges, and foothills—wherever work was planned. Spike camps were often established when work was far from camp. For example, a Camp Paradise spike camp was established at the Reno Airport during construction of a Forest Service warehouse. High-elevation camps in Lamoille Canyon and Mount Charleston were seasonal by necessity. During the winter, enrollees were routinely relocated to camps in warmer or lower-elevation areas like Camp Paradise or Camp Wells Siding (Logandale). In severe winters, however, even high valley camps were confronted with logistical problems. During the winter of 1936–1937, the year-round Reese River camp (forty-three miles from Austin) miraculously escaped tragedy when temperatures dipped to forty-three degrees below zero. The rural camp was snowbound for weeks and eventually ran out of coal to heat the barracks. The resourceful men managed to stay warm by burning sagebrush and wil-

A Camp Reese River crew clears loose rock from the bank of a newly constructed road over Ione Summit, 1937. Courtesy Edna Timmons

low branches. It is probably no coincidence that Camp Reese River sat empty for the next three years. A "Camp Inspection Report" for February 1937 documented the two-month ordeal:

> The Forestry Service has had their hands full with emergency calls from outside camp. . . . [O]ne little "Cat" has worked steady day and night to keep us in touch with the world. The train which usually brings supplies to us has been snowbound for the past 40 days somewhere between Austin and Battle Mountain. All and all we have had a real experience which the boys can never forget when they return to their homes in Ohio and Kentucky.[26]

Other than the extreme weather, the CCC experience in northern Nye County was positive overall. Ranger districts, stockmen, miners, and residents of the nearby Yomba Indian Reservation were especially grateful for the new roads that provided reliable access to their area. The Nye County Commission was optimistic that the road work completed with CCC labor would allow year-round travel and stimulate new mining ventures.[27] A 75-man spike camp was established in Manhattan during road improvements from the reservation through Cloverdale, connecting with the Smoky Valley Highway and northward through Belmont and Northumberland. The enrollees were housed in the historic Nye County Courthouse in Belmont while constructing the sixteen-foot forest regulation highway between Belmont and Monitor Valley.[28]

The Reese River camp reopened in 1941. Not surprisingly, the 105 replacements from Georgia were leary of the harsh winters and the camp's rural location. The CCC camp inspector also had doubts: "Will be surprised if those enrollees from the South, will remain here, unless, many past-times are carried on in camp." In contrast, sixty Camp Paradise enrollees, displeased with the Camp Paradise administration, were happy to be transferred to Camp Reese River. Apparently, the camp surgeon and junior officer had just been dismissed for habitual drunkenness and drinking with enrollees. Camp morale suffered, and a spike camp was shut down for shoddy conditions.[29] Unfortunately, the lackadaisical attitude at Camp Paradise was not an isolated incident. Maintaining high morale and full companies was a growing challenge in Nevada and around the country toward the end of the CCC program.

Despite growing desertion rates, most Forest Service programs achieved high marks. One successful program was at Camp Charleston Mountain. It could be said that Camp Charleston Mountain was southern Nevada's counterpart to Camp Lamoille. CCC inspector M. J. Bowen praised the camp and the scenery in a 1937 "Camp Inspection Report":

> Work Projects: All work projects located on Charleston Mt., [camp elevation] 8,000 feet . . . 35 miles from Los [*sic*] Vegas and a beautiful place. Some three or four thousand people visit this play and camping ground [on] weekends. [Tasks include] such work as public camp ground development, parking areas, developing water, tables, benches, fire places, and constructing 3 miles of road (heavy) to the summit. A splendid skiing site has also been developed for winter sports. Until the arrival of the CCC, four years ago, this place was almost unheard of. . . . Any boy who could not stay in this camp during the summer . . . could not fit in a CCC camp.[30]

A 1938 supplemental "Camp Inspection Report" for Camp Charleston Mountain discussed enrollees' good behavior and Company 5441's southern origins:

> The camp is educationally minded. . . . A few enrollees complained concerning the lack of variety in menus, particularly meat and the lack of fresh fruits. Beef in

Men from Company 1530 salute the flag at Camp Charleston Mountain. The camp was situated in pine-covered Kyle Canyon, northwest of Las Vegas. Courtesy California Conservation Corps Museum

> some form has been rather regular, but the heat of Las Vegas, the procuring point, which has extremely hot weather . . . furnishes the risk of spoilage in certain other kinds of meat. . . . Chicken served was criticized for lack of meat. The Fourth Corps boys are accustomed to fried chicken. The class of chickens possible under stipulated contracts in the Ninth Corps does not provide for fryers. . . . Either a member of the camp personnel, or a leader, says grace before each meal, which I believe is unusual for a CCC Camp. Past members of the enrollee personnel have been almost entirely Protestant. . . . [M]uch is said in favor of the enrollees from that section of the country.[31]

Mount Charleston's new recreation facilities generated their share of national interest. You might say that the excitement of Hoover Dam spilled over on the forest park. The Kyle Canyon Campgrounds represented the largest and most heavily visited campsite in the Nevada forests.[32] Undoubtedly, Mount Charleston's most distinguished visitors were President and Mrs. Franklin D. Roosevelt who visited the recreation area following the dedication of Hoover (then Boulder) Dam in 1935. Had the dedication occurred a year later, the president would have witnessed the CCC program in action--unfortunately, the presidential visit occurred during the one year that Camp Charleston Mountain was closed. Nonetheless, the president and first lady were able to observe WPA and transient workers engaged in the construction of Harris Springs Road in Kyle Canyon.[33]

By the spring of 1936, the CCC continued where they left off in 1934. Crews built a water system for the Kyle Canyon Campground, the Rainbow Canyon summer-home area, the Kyle Canyon Guard Station, and the Air Force Base Rest Camp. Considerable time was also spent cleaning up collapsed CCC barracks destroyed by devastating storms during the previous winter. Unfortunately, the replacement tents were old and leaked. A second tent had to be draped over the top to keep rain out.[34] Once the camp was operational, the CCC began constructing Deer Creek Road into Lee Canyon and building trails to Little Falls and Mount Baldy.[35]

With the goal of creating a winter wonderland in southern Nevada, the plans for a ski jump, ski run, skate pond, and toboggan slide at Kyle Canyon were soon under way. Champion skier and Olympic coach Alf Engen served as the winter sports adviser for Utah, Nevada, and Idaho. Engen's involvement was crucial. He and forest supervisor George Larson spent long days on-site and personally supervised the construction of the snow park.[36]

By the early 1940s, even Camp Charleston Mountain could not escape the nationwide downtrend in the CCC program. In contrast to the camp's early momentum, the men in Company 5441 were unmotivated and suffered from an inept camp commander. A "Camp Inspection Report" dated June 10, 1942, reflects the substandard conditions: "General camp conditions, very unsatisfactory; including morale, and mess; Boys very untidy, slack, and unkempt. . . . Enrollees not up to general average of enrollees." The sad state of affairs was undoubtedly fostered by the commander's chronic absences, heavy drinking, and habit of bringing intoxicated women back to the camp. After leaving his CCC job for regular army duty, the commander's replacement had little time to turn conditions around before the CCC program ended two months later.[37]

As the demise of the CCC program neared, the Forest Service escalated

CCC work projects along the eastern Sierra Nevada, in western Nevada. Still, the program at Camp Galena was modest in comparison to the large programs at Camps Paradise, Lamoille, and Charleston Mountain. Camp Galena's history remains somewhat vague, and its records are hard to locate.[38] Although the *Reno Evening Gazette* covered the Camp Galena Creek's fifth anniversary celebration in March 21, 1940, it is difficult to establish the camp strength due to forest reorganization. Camp Galena's jurisdiction was transferred from the Tahoe National Forest to the Mono National Forest during the CCC years.[39] Originally built as a transient camp, the Galena facility was reused by the WPA before becoming a Forest Service CCC camp. The men of Camp Galena (assisted by the WPA) built a ski hut on Galena Creek, a ski trail for the University of Nevada ski team, and a stone fish hatchery at Galena State Park.[40] A mobile spike camp in Verdi installed check dams to control bank erosion and construct drift fences along the California-Nevada state line in Dog Valley.[41] As a final assignment, the camp was responsible for constructing and operating the CCC Central Repair Shop on East Second Street in Reno. Although a Forest Service project, the facility was built to service CCC vehicles from all agencies. With a twenty-man staff, it was reputedly one of the best-equipped CCC machine shops in the country.[42] Years later, the land on East Second Street was sold to the Washoe Medical Center.[43]

Several of Camp Galena's projects were performed with the help of Camp Antelope (F-396) nearby in Coleville, California. Also administered by the Mono National Forest, Camp Antelope enrollees frequently worked in western Nevada. They eventually remodeled the former armory building in Carson City to house a spike camp of forty to fifty men. The two camps are credited with constructing a telephone line from Carson City to Glenbrook at Lake Tahoe and improving the McClellan Peak–Incline power line. Camp Antelope also constructed the administrative buildings at the Wellington Ranger Station (now privately owned) and initiated the construction of the Carson District Ranger headquarters in Carson City.[44]

By the end of the CCC program, most camps were dismantled, although others were reused for different purposes. Camp Coleville subsumed the Camp Antelope facility on the east side of Antelope Valley and became the home of conscientious objectors from across the nation. The men picked up where Grazing Service enrollees left off and opted to work on range improvements in lieu of bearing arms.[45]

Men from Camp Galena Creek and the WPA constructed the stone ski hut on the east slope of Mount Rose. Courtesy Humboldt-Toiyabe National Forest

Edmund Rosowski, Camps Paradise, Lamoille, and Reese River

At the time I went in the three-Cs, both my parents were deceased, and I lived with my sister in Orchard Park, New York, . . . thirty miles south of Buffalo. . . . I graduated from a Franciscan-run high school. . . . They were recruiting CCs [*sic*] to go West. It was advertised in the *Buffalo Evening News*. . . . I went in and was accepted. . . .

Somewhere the rumor came up that we were going to Nevada, but where in Nevada, I had no idea. . . . We pulled into Winnemucca, and then we were loaded onto trucks. At that time, they were called stake-body, which is a flat truck with benches inside and a canvas cover over the top. They all had Forest Service emblems on them. . . . We traveled about forty miles north to Paradise Valley. . . . I was surprised. I was pretty happy with the surroundings. That's a beautiful area. . . . I never found any antagonism from people in Winnemucca. They liked the extra money, I guess, that was coming into town. . . .

My job, basically, was with trucks. I was tested and assigned a truck to drive. . . . [T]he job I was concerned with . . . as a truck driver was making roads. . . . CCC crews would go out and make roads into the mountains, as perhaps a route to go in case of a fire. In other words, we were making roads up canyons.

The trucks were mostly three-quarter or half-ton, small Chevrolets, which used to blow the axles very easily. . . . If you let out the clutch too soon with a heavy load, you just stood there, because you probably broke one of the axles. And then somebody had to come in, which finally turned out to be my job. . . . I was changed from ordinary truck driver [to] a truck master . . . two or three months after I was in. . . . So I was assigned a pickup. I carried extra axles. . . . I could repair basic problems, although we did have mechanics in the crews that did actually repair those vehicles. . . . Mr. Timmons . . . was in charge of the garage [and] . . . my immediate supervisor.[46]

Do you have any idea what a drift fence is? That was one of the jobs. . . . They would go out and repair drift fences for cattle control. . . . When we were resupplied . . . with new recruits . . . very often you had to teach some of the city people how to use a shovel. . . . They actually didn't know how to throw dirt. . . .

Most of the work I did was to haul fence posts from the lower part of Utah . . . south of Salt Lake City. It was the Desert Range Experimental Station Farm, where they experimented with grass that could survive long droughts. . . . They were cedar scrub trees; however, they were straight enough for at least seven or eight feet and made a very good fence post. That's what we used in those drift fences. . . . When we were on the road, we were allowed per diem . . . either two and a half or three dollars a day. . . . For the gasoline . . . we would stop at various other CCC camps and resupply the fuel for the trucks. . . .

I didn't stay in Paradise Valley all of the time. We moved the camp . . . two other times. . . . There was [Camp Reese River] . . . that we occupied for six or seven months. . . . Then we moved up to Elko. . . . to a place called Lamoille. . . . In fact, the time that we were there, in Jiggs, Nevada, they filmed the cricket scenes for that Mormon movie. I forgot what the name of it was.

At Lamoille, it was either firefighting or road construction. . . . I remember one of the jobs I had was hauling dynamite for blasting the roads off the side of the mountain. I used to haul it from the boxcars at Elko and haul it to camp. . . . I used to haul on the back of that big trailer . . . to rangers' stations that had horses.

Medical Care

I remember Dr. Anderson at Paradise Valley. He was quite a gentleman. . . . [W]e had an ambulance that would take any severe patients to a hospital. . . . [T]hey did take some people as far as Sacramento . . . because there was an army hospital there . . .[47]

Recreation

We had dances at camp sponsored by the CCC, and we would go into . . . Winnemucca and bring girls out. And it was strictly chaperoned. Those dances would probably go until about eleven o'clock, and then, they would be back home by midnight. . . . There was one chaperone for every girl. . . . Winnemucca used to have a rodeo, and we would bring the citizens from the camp over for a day of rodeo. The camp had a baseball team, and they would play local high school teams.

I came home in the fall of 1941 . . . and then I got drafted the following Easter. . . . I volunteered for parachutes, and I became a paratrooper, and we shipped to Africa. . . . Most of my operations were in the invasion of Sicily, where I got hurt and that was the end of me. . . .

I think the CCC helped me, because I got promoted to sergeant in the army, and I signed up to go to . . . officers training. . . . I got shipped out before that. . . . After the war I came home partly disabled, so I went to college, got a bachelor's degree in accounting and a master's degree in education, and then I taught high school.[48]

11

Controlling Erosion Along Nevada Waterways

The CCC and the Soil Conservation Service

Persistent droughts and a series of floods took their toll on Nevada's agriculture industry in the 1930s and early 1940s. Erosion was a statewide problem, although the situation was most severe along the lower Colorado River watersheds in southern Nevada. Historically, major floods ravaged the region about every fifteen years with smaller episodes in between.[1] All too often, farmers living along the Meadow Valley Wash and the Muddy and Virgin Rivers watched helplessly while rich farmland was carried downstream and gullies widened. The Union Pacific's Los Angeles and Salt Lake Railroad line also suffered frequent losses. On several occasions, segments of the line through Rainbow Canyon near Caliente washed out, causing millions of dollars of damage and cessation of rail service.[2] The Union Pacific's line through the lower Moapa Valley was also frequently damaged. Discouraged farmers knew that something had to be done to save their farms and ranches.

A young Nevada Extension Service agent, Louie Gardella, recalled the dismal conditions in Lincoln County in 1934:

> There were several things that played in creating the attitude and the depressing atmosphere and the beaten outlook that the ranchers and farmers and everybody had . . . but it was particularly bad in that section of Lincoln and Clark counties. . . . I'll just describe the conditions that was down on . . . the Meadow Valley Wash, south of Caliente. There were eight or ten so-called ranches down there, just small places. And they were so blamed poor and the resources weren't there. . . . I saw once an old man . . . a fine old man, too. And he had a team of mules . . . and he had a sled that he drug around. He was pulling down these big barrel cactuses, he threw a chain around 'em and pulled 'em over, and gathered some brush and he'd burn the spikes off of 'em. And then he had a saw and hatchet, and he'd cut the outer pulp off of 'em and throw it into the sled and hauled it up to his corral where he was feeding about twenty-five head of cows, cattle that were in very bad shape because we were in drought. And this was the only feed that he could furnish them.[3]

Plans for flood control began several years earlier, when John H. Wittwer became the district extension agent for Clark and Lincoln Counties. While standing at the confluence of the Meadow Valley Wash and Muddy River, he realized that the floodwaters that raced past him originated nearly one hundred miles to the north in the Meadow Valley Wash watersheds.[4] The insightful agent convinced commissioners from Clark and Lincoln Counties of the need for a comprehensive flood-control study. In 1927, the engineering firm of King and Malone was hired by the Muddy Valley Irrigation Company to begin the study. The engineers recommended a series of dams, weirs, and spillways along headwaters and tributaries of the Muddy River drainage and the Clark County portion of the Meadow Valley Wash. The study was later expanded to include the upper Meadow Valley Wash and the Virgin River drainage near Mesquite.[5]

Fortunately, federal funding for erosion control became available following the famous dust-bowl incident in the southern Midwest. The resulting National Industrial Recovery Act (NIRA) created the Soil Erosion Service (SES) in 1933. The SES oversaw soil erosion programs and immediately took advantage of CCC labor to help with its mission. The SES was restructured under the Department of Agriculture following passage of the Soil Conservation Act of 1935. The act created the Soil Conservation Service (SCS). The SCS continued to use CCC and WPA labor to develop its experimental stations and nurseries.[6] State conservation districts administered federal conservation programs at the local level. Working together, the SCS and conservation districts developed work plans to implement much-needed flood-control measures.

Five SES/SCS CCC camps tackled the erosion problem in southern Nevada; a sixth camp was later established south of Gardnerville to straighten sharp bends and stabilize banks along the east fork of the Carson River.[7] Three private flood-control projects (Panaca, Bunkerville, and Wells Siding) are included in this discussion. Two of these projects were later administered by the SCS. The first southern Nevada camps were established in the upper Moapa Valley and at Ash Springs in Pahranagat Valley. Before long, camps were built in Panaca, Bunkerville, and Pioche. Camp Wells Siding in Logandale is included in this chapter since it was the largest flood-control project in the state. While the SCS provided some technical advice for the Wells Siding–Bowman Reservoir Project, the private undertaking was actually supervised by the Forest Service. Similarly, the Forest Service supervised early SCS projects in Panaca and the Alamo and Hiko areas. This arrangement between the Forest Service and the SCS was maintained for most of the CCC years. While the Forest Service directed the work, the SCS provided project specifications and developed work plans. Local conservation districts usually provided the funding and construction materials.

SCS projects were usually on private land, in keeping with the SCS's mission to help landowners. For other agencies, however, the protocol for using CCC labor on private land was less clear, and the public-private issue was the subject of ongoing debate.[8]

But the SCS mission was unique, and erosion-control work on private land was deemed necessary in the public interest. There was plenty of work to be done. The Camp Caliente enrollees began one of their first projects in the upper extremities of the Meadow Valley Wash. To slow floodwaters and catch debris, a series of dams, dikes, and spillways were strategically placed along the wash and side drainages near Hogon, Alamo, and Hiko.[9] Despite some immediate relief, significant damages were sustained during one well-documented flood that ravaged the area on March 3–5, 1938. Streambanks suffered major erosion, and Caliente roads, highways, and bridges were washed away. To the south, Bunkerville's irrigation system was destroyed, and its freshwater supply polluted. For Well Siding superintendent Jim Griswold, the flood was the largest that he had ever seen in this area. Still, the towns of Overton and Logandale fared considerably better than upstream communities because of the Wells Siding–Bowman Reservoir Project. Griswold was pleased, albeit cautious, about the new flood-control system:

> It is the consensus of opinion of the people in Moapa Valley and also the Forest Overhead at the CCC Camp at Wells Siding that the flood control works were instrumental in confining the water and preventing a great amount of damage to farms and homes in the valley. Much credit can be given to the CCC boys who worked day and night to control the floodwater. Out of it all comes the unmistakable lesson that the flood control works must be enlarged and strengthened if they are to handle such floods in the future.[10]

Yearly floods also played havoc on the town of Panaca. Water flowing through the Panaca Wash often damaged the schoolhouse and residences. To avert future flood damage, Camp Panaca men set out to divert floodwaters around the town. The construction of an 12,590-foot earthen dike and a mile-long canal around the outskirts of town provided some comfort to

fearful Panaca residents. The Panaca Project is characterized by eight rock-rubble masonry spillways and concrete drops excavated by tractors and horse teams. Other rock-rubble and concrete-drop dams were built northeast of town in Eagle and Rose Valleys. To prevent road washouts along the Panaca-Modena Highway (State Route 319), a 65-foot bridge was constructed over the new flood-control structures. Despite good intentions, many of the Panaca area flood-control projects were short-lived due to poor engineering and the use of unsuitable building materials. Extension agent Gardella was one of the few who sensed the problems ahead:

> They started to put in three [drop] dams in Rose Valley. And they decided they would put in what they call log crib dams or rock crib dams. That is, they went off and they cut a lot of . . . cedar posts . . . and then made a kind of cribbing and then filled it in with rock and put it in the creek. . . . And the water would flow through that and wouldn't wash the sides and then they put dikes on either side, going off to the side of the valley, so it forced all the water over the dam. To do this, they didn't know the amount of water that came down, or the size of the creek, or how they should build them. . . . They decided that the width of the drop dams should be cut down by about approximately half. I said "No, that won't do; you're going to get some trouble." . . . The first flood that came down took all three dams, because the spillways weren't large enough. So, they redesigned the dam and they put in, actually, four . . . concrete drop dams: three in Rose Valley and one at the end of Eagle Valley. . . . I think that they are still there yet.[11]

Hard lessons were learned, and most subsequent projects withstood the tests of time. One example is the Mathews Drop Dam (northeast of Caliente) built in 1938 to stop gully erosion along the Meadow Valley Wash. It immediately slowed head-cutting by slowing the force of floodwaters. Over time, sediments built up behind the dam and the Panaca Meadows gradually replaced the wide gully that once dissected the valley. Similarly, the fer-

---

Opposite, top. Camp Panaca constructed several rock-filled gabions along the banks of the Meadow Valley Wash in Rose Valley. Courtesy Natural Resource Conservation Service

Opposite, bottom. Floods along the Meadow Valley Wash frequently destroyed bridges, roads, and buildings in their path. Caliente residents watch helplessly as a major flood ripped through their town in 1938. Courtesy Natural Resource Conservation Service tile meadows in Eagle and Rose Valleys were salvaged by rock-masonry drop dams built in the 1930s.[12]

There was more flood-control work to be done in valleys to the west. Camp Caliente crews installed flood-control drain-pipe and water-diversion structures from the lower Alamo Lake north to Hiko in Pahranagat Valley. In those days, Pahranagat Valley was extremely boggy and impassable due to continuous runoff from Ash, Crystal, and Hiko Springs.[13] In addition to active spring flow, the valley was frequently inundated from summer downpours in the hills above Alamo and Hiko. Through a combination of manual labor, steam shovels, and horse teams, the CCC dug channels and built dikes to divert torrential waters around the town of Alamo. Local farmer Joe Higbee remembers watching the CCC enrollees manually haul dirt and large rocks out of the large channel. He also recalls the childhood admiration he had for the young men with the strong backs and dark tans.[14]

Frequent floods washed away the richest soils and threatened the livelihood of stockmen and farmers living along the Meadow Valley Wash. A Soil Conservation Service agent assessed the ever-widening gully north of Panaca, 1936. Courtesy Natural Resource Conservation Service

The CCC built the Mathews Drop Dam north of Caliente. The dam was intended to slow floodwaters and stop head-cutting along this portion of the Meadow Valley Wash. The Panaca Meadows eventually replaced the huge channel that nearly ruined this valley. Courtesy Natural Resource Conservation Service

The public was encouraged to visit the multitude of CCC-built projects in Pahranagat Valley. These include the Alamo and Cox flood-control levy, the catchment basin for a ten-square-mile area, and the earth-filled Frehner, Hiko, Pahranagat, and Cox Dykes.[15] The CCC excavated and installed an extensive system of tile drains and pipe to lower the water table so crops such as corn and alfalfa could flourish in once saturated fields. Farmers were pleased when swampy fields were transformed into productive farmland near Richardville and on the Martin Bunker Ranch near Alamo.[16]

Meanwhile, projects in the lower Moapa Valley were in full swing. Efforts to control floods originating upstream in the Meadow Valley Wash and upper Muddy River basin required an integrated system of flood-control dams and spillways along the Muddy River.[17] Projects included the rock-masonry Arrowhead Dam built in Arrow Canyon, fifteen miles from Moapa, and the Glendale Flood Control Works at the confluence of the Meadow Valley

Wash and the Muddy River near the town of Glendale. The CCC Indian Department program also built three dams on the Moapa Indian Reservation: the earth and rock-filled White Narrows Dam on the Muddy River Channel, the Hogans Wash Dam on a Muddy River tributary, and a "South Dam" in between.[18] Despite collective efforts, a 1939 flood originating in the upper watershed of the Muddy River inundated the Home Ranch and drowned agricultural fields on the reservation.

The lower Moapa Valley was more fortunate that year as a result of the newly enlarged flood channel of the Wells Siding–Bowman Reservoir Project.[19] In previous years, residents had not been so lucky. In the spring of 1936, rising waters flooded homes near Overton and threatened to carry others away. CCC men worked tirelessly, evacuating residents to higher ground, and opening windows and doors to let the water flow through. Though grateful that their homes were saved, home owners complained that the smell of the flood never went away.[20]

The privately funded Wells Siding–Bowman Reservoir Project was financed by the Muddy Valley Irrigation Company and the Moapa Soil Conservation District. The project was intended to protect the lower Moapa Valley's thirty-seven hundred acres of arable land from further flood damage and erosion. The massive flood-control works were composed of several integrated components: a diversion and storage dam at Wells Siding, a storage dam at Bowman Basin (originally built for flood control, its capacity was increased from one thousand to four thousand acre-feet in 1968), a flood channel with canals and levees to connect the two dams, a three thousand–second-foot spillway at Wells Siding Dam, a four thousand–second-foot spillway channel at Wells Siding Dam, a bypass outlet for normal flow of the Muddy River, a slide headgate control (Triple Gates) at the entrance to the flood channel, a fifty-seven-foot timber highway bridge at the state highway crossing, and a safety spillway in the channel behind Bowman Reservoir.[21] Enrollees on this project gained valuable experience working on a public works project of this complexity.

The Forest Service continued to supervise SCS flood-control projects in Nevada throughout most of the CCC program. However, in 1940 a change in the U.S. Department of Agriculture's policy threatened the future of this arrangement. Due to a favorable working relationship, it was not surprising that the Moapa Soil Conservation District fought to maintain Forest Service supervision over the Wells Siding–Bowman Reservoir Project. A letter

Camp Wells Siding was assigned to flood-control work in the lower Moapa Valley. This four thousand–foot-per-second rock spillway is one component of the massive Wells Siding–Bowman Reservoir Project built in 1934–1935. Courtesy Humboldt-Toiyabe National Forest

from Cecil Creel to J. H. Wittwer addressed the compromises made to accommodate the district:

> The Secretary of Agriculture had signed the letter addressed to Mr. Marshall [Moapa Soil Conservation District] relative to the Department's plans for handling the Wells Siding Camp. I . . . understand that it provides for operation of the camp under the present Forest Service Personnel in accordance with agreements reached between the District, the Soil Conservation, and the Forest Service. The General Department policy now is to have all CCC flood control and Soil Conservation work, including drainage, I believe, taken care of by SCS camps. An exception is being made, partially, at least in Department policy, to meet the wishes of the local people.[22]

A day later, Senator McCarran sent a Western Union telegram to Edwin Marshall clarifying the new arrangement: "Have succeeded in retaining Forest Service control of personnel and actual operation of camp. Soil Conservation will determine work program and specification due to mature project but will in no way interfere with advantages to be secured from handling of detail by Forest Service."[23]

At the same time that communities along the Muddy River and Meadow Valley Wash fought to save agricultural land, the small communities of Bunkerville and Mesquite near the Utah border waged a similar battle. Here, the SCS was directly involved in helping struggling farmers in Virgin Valley. The Bunkerville CCC men spent three seasons fighting bank erosion, repairing flood damage, and slowing the loss of rich bottomland along the Virgin River. In 1934 alone, Bunkerville enrollees built twenty-two rock barriers along drainages and planted twelve thousand tree cuttings to stabilize the riverbank and slow channel movement.[24] Working alongside residents, the CCC helped secure a clean source of water from the Virgin Mountains. With funding from the Mormon Church and the SCS, the CCC and residents constructed several miles of pipeline to bring water from Cabin Spring to a storage tank on the alluvial slope above town. For years, residents drove eight miles up the hill to haul fresh water from this tank until a new facility was built.[25]

Townspeople were appreciative of the help that they received from the program. According to one newspaper, the SCS's CCC program "met a demand for protection which the local people could not meet."[26] The Soil Conservation Service's CCC program was acknowledged by announcer Charles Jarrett during a *Western Farm and Home Hour* radio program in 1937:

> With only one acre out of 15 for raising crops, and those acres going fast due to river bank erosion, it's little wonder that the citizens of Nevada have welcomed the work of the Soil Conservation Service at Bunkerville and other places. They were a great bunch of men. And by the way, the C.C.C. enrollees here in Nevada have been saving more than soil this past winter. They have been saving lives. I heard them talking about it last night—fighting snowdrifts head deep to break trail to bands of starving sheep and cattle. Once during this past winter an emergency call came in asking for a tractor to break trail into a herd of sheep that was snowbound near Sand Springs. . . . They not only saved a band of sheep that time, but on the way they came across two miners who had been living on jackrabbits and flour for two weeks.[27]

As was the practice in southern Nevada, Bunkerville enrollees were transferred to other camps during the hot summer months. But even in the spring, the Virgin River could be a safety hazard to enrollees working unprotected in the hot sun. As a CCC requirement, sun damage and restrictions for swimming during working hours were discussed during a March 9, 1937, safety meeting:

> Capt. Fowler mentioned that there was a regulation against swimming while on duty. . . . Dr. Anderson warned that it would be well to observe the enrollees for sun stroke or heat stroke and explained the proper treatment for anyone having symptoms of these ailments. Also he said that snakes would have to be watched now that the sun was getting warm and that scorpions, while being poisonous, were not ordinarily fatal. Leaders and assistant leaders were once more warned to watch enrollees to see that they did not try to get a tan to [*sic*] quickly.[28]

Although the Virgin River flood-control measures helped temporarily, few withstood the test of time. The water system's iron pipeline has since been replaced, and more substantial flood-resistant dams were constructed where rock and wire dams once protected the valley's three ditch systems.[29] Today, there are few physical reminders of the CCC in Virgin Valley, but local biographies documented their contributions:

> Early summer of 1938 storm and flood washed out all of irrigation ditch and [Mesquite] dam. As town was repairing damage another flood caused more major damage. People of Bunkerville so exhausted and discouraged they asked counsel from Church leaders in Salt Lake City, Utah. Apostle Melvin Ballard came and surveyed damage and counseled the people of Bunkerville to abandon the town and move elsewhere. People refused. People sought help from Nevada's U.S. Senator Pat McCarran and the CCC boys moved into town and within two days 200 men with trucks and heavy equipment arrived to repair dam and canal. Six weeks later water was in the ditch.[30]

Another source described other aspects of the flood. This account describes the severe damage to dams and crops:

> It took out the [Mesquite] dam, filled up the tunnel at the intake of the canal and washed away the head of the canal into the hill for 100 yards, also washed away the canal at what is know as Tunnel Point, leaving a perpendicular bank of 130 feet high. It has also taken away the dams at Bunkerville and nearby ranches and did much damage to their canals. It will take at least a month to six weeks with all the local help and the help available from the CCC to put the water back into canal in time to save the crops.[31]

In recent decades, larger better-engineered dams have replaced earlier structures on the Meadow Valley Wash and the Muddy and Virgin Rivers. Although the flood-control work is ongoing, the first serious attempts to gain control of southern Nevada's rivers and channels were made possible by New Deal monies and programs such as the CCC. With free labor, the early structures were built at proportionately lower costs at a time when money was scarce.[32] Structures such as the Mathews Drop Dam continue to perform as originally intended.[33] Still, the crumbling concrete, protruding rebar, and eroding levees are signs that major repairs or replacements are needed. Today, government officials creatively look for ways to finance the aging flood-control systems in lieu of today's high cost of materials and labor. Only this time around, there will be no help from the CCC.

Elmer R. Randall, Educational Adviser, Camp Panaca and Camp Indian Springs

---

When I entered the CCC program, I had been principal of Virgin Valley High School, and my wife didn't like the Virgin Valley. You know, the temperature could reach 120 degrees. . . . We had to haul our water in from five miles further east in a fifteen-hundred-gallon tank. Then we'd dump it in a cistern, and then we had to go back and get another one. . . . And if you wanted electricity after seven o'clock, you had to go make arrangement with . . . Nate Abbott. And if you wanted it before seven, well, you had another argument with him.

I just quit. . . . I moved my wife and the kids up to the cabin and parked them with her folks in Idaho. . . . Someone over by Montpelier, Idaho . . . offered me a job. I said, "No, I have an application in for the CCCs, and I expect that to come in before long, and I don't want to go up to your school if I can only stay a month or six weeks." He says, "Well, you come on out, and when you have to go, we'll release you." I guess it was in October [1940] that my application went through and was approved, and so I loaded up my three kids and my wife and headed out . . . to Panaca. I was the education adviser, but I did everything [laughter]. I made it so nobody else wanted the job.

I taught reading, writing, and math to boys from Tennessee, South Carolina—kids that couldn't get a job anywhere, and these guys were a little young to go in the army. . . . We didn't have a big facility, and I . . . had to give them some fundamentals, you know. I had control of the kids: if I said they didn't go out on a recreation trip, they didn't go, because they weren't studying.

I taught in the afternoon, if there was some students there, and evenings every day. . . . Well, Thursday night was our recreation night, and we had two places to go: one was Caliente, and the other one was Pioche. . . . They had homesickness. . . . most of them were under twenty years old, you know.

They would sass their people and truckers. I had two or three assistant educational advisers that I had appointed, so they were directly under me. If I didn't like what the student was doing to these assistants, they got rapped.

I liked the CCC camps for the freedom from people looking over your shoulder. I got fifty kids out there looking over the fence, and I got fifty mothers and fathers back in Tennessee, and that's where I wanted them [laughter]. I knew what I wanted to do, and I know how to do it right, so I did it. In schools, you might not have such good luck.

There were about sixty guys in our camp, and at the spike camp at Alamo, we had about ten or fifteen men, who were out of our home camp, and we had about twenty down back in Virgin Valley, Bunkerville, my hometown.

. . . I am sure that the town appreciated what the CCC boys did after they got to seeing the effect of it. . . .

This was the last seven months or so of this camp at Panaca: it closed at the end of June in 1941. Then we went up to Ely . . . at the Indian Springs Camp [at Moorman Ranch]. . . . Now the situation was this with Indian Springs: Three educational advisers in the area—that included me—were all sent there at the same time. . . . So we just sat down and looked at each other for three days. I thought I wasn't going to get to stay, because I'd been on the job only about seven months. But I traded something at the main office in Salt Lake City. In about a week . . . orders come through . . . to turn over their records to me and take their leave of absence. Effectively, they were fired.

Maybe a half a dozen was trying to learn to read. Then some of them studied a little mathematics, but none of them got too far. In the first place, I didn't start school till two-thirty in the afternoon. . . . I helped start the camp at Moorman [Ranch]. We started out living in tents, but not for long. When you got sixty guys carrying the wood, you can build cabins pretty fast [laughter]. . . . My family was there with me because I had a travel trailer . . . I built while I was in Virgin Valley. I had one classroom that we didn't use, so I took that over. It was my carpenter shop, and I built this travel trailer inside. . . . I wasn't there very long [laughter]. I heard that there was a superintendency up in Firth, Idaho. . . . So I got right in the car and took off for Firth.[34]

12

The CCC Legacy in Nevada

More than seventy years have passed since the founding of the Civilian Conservation Corps. Most Nevadans do not remember the contributions of these young men or the how the Great Depression affected the rural state. We rarely question who carved out the backcountry roads, lined the canals, or built the campgrounds with signature rock walls, fire pits, and park trails that we use and enjoy today. Many New Deal projects have disappeared or are showing their age, although the basic foundations of Nevada's early recreational facilities, wildlife preserves, and irrigation systems have withstood the test of time.

Fortunately, historians and historic preservationists have a renewed interest in the Depression era, and Nevadans are eager to reacquaint themselves with the events of this period. Thus, the CCC legacy will not be forgotten. The struggle to survive the adversity of the 1930s constitutes another major chapter in America's heritage. Oral historians seek the personal stories of CCC alumni, many of whom are esteemed veterans of World War II.

Looking back, it is difficult to assess the true value of the CCC contribution to Nevada without placing it in the context of the New Deal. We will never know how Nevadans would have fared without aid from the federal government. It is clear that New Dealers looked favorably on Nevada. Federal monies eased the symptoms of the Depression and made life a little easier. And although the environment benefited from the New Deal, the improvements to land and municipal structures were by-products, rather than objectives, of the massive economic recovery effort. FDR's overriding goal was to provide hope for discouraged Americans; the main goal of his CCC program was to save a generation of unmarried young men. For the president, creating jobs for working-age males superceded all else. These men were our future. But FDR considered the well-being of all Americans. While young men worked on conservation projects, others were put to work on capital developments.[1] Although New Deal programs like social security, farm price supports, securities and bank regulations, and minimum-wage legislation have survived, those that provided employment ended with the economic recovery enticed by World War II.

Nevada received the largest per capita allotment of New Deal monies in the nation because of its huge federal landholdings and influential public officials. According to the national CCC director's estimate, the CCC "advanced range rehabilitation by ten to twenty years."[2] But this attention to the land would not last. The demands of a global war undermined the progress made in the 1930s. Range-management controls on public domain and forestlands stalled, and no new reclamation projects were planned. As summed up by one historian, FDR's conservation momentum soon became a nonissue on the American agenda.[3]

The abrupt cessation of federal support affected land managers and citizens alike. For nine years, the CCC served as the main search-and-rescue team, firefighters, and civil defense squad. Not surprisingly, the CCC program was sorely missed. Derrel Fulwider, a forty-two-year veteran with the U.S. Forest Service and Bureau of Land Management, described the challenges land managers faced:

> The year 1942 was very bad for fires. The CCCs had previously been used on fire suppression work. So there was no district fire organization when I came into the [Winnemucca] District in February of that year. . . . Two fires in July and August in the Buffalo Hills–Painter Flat area burned some 345,000 acres. . . . Truckloads of transients were rounded up in Reno. . . . [A]nyone interested in making a buck, including jailbirds, were brought to Winnemucca. . . . It was also noted . . . how important previous fire suppression work by the CCCs had been, as well as other work . . . like building roads. . . . Most of the firefighters that year were winos.[4]

The situation at Hawthorne was equally grim. Without the CCC to build new roads and improve the Naval Ammunition Depot, the search for reliable workers for wartime expansion turned out to be a challenge. Accountant Austin Childs had little recourse but to hire a "rougher class from the Eastern cities of Detroit, Cleveland . . . bums, petty criminals and undesirables."[5]

Despite thousands of improvements made to the Nevada landscape, the enrollees reaped the greatest benefits. For nine years, the federal government had taken responsibility for this generation of young men. Though it was a tough transition for some, the militaristic lifestyle was superior to the plight of migrant workers who "squatted" on government land or the precarious existence of hoboes who hopped trains in search of casual work. CCC training continued to help the men long after their discharge from the program. Enrollees inducted into the armed forces adapted far more easily than recruits new to a regimented lifestyle. Most of the men were thankful to have three square meals a day, honest work, and shelter. Chaplain Robert L. Dougherty of Camp Newlands, Company 4743, expressed the men's gratitude during a Thanksgiving Day blessing:

> We live in the richest and freest country on earth. Every opportunity is ours to climb to the heights of our fondest dreams, if we are willing to work and sacrifice. Let us make this day more than a feast day, may we truly be grateful to our nation that gives us our chance; to our government for the privileges we enjoy in the Civilian Conservation Corps; to Almighty God for the material and spiritual blessings so abundantly bestowed on us![6]

As expected with any politically sponsored program, improvements to the health and well-being of enrollees were heavily politicized by government officials. The testimonies of alumni and CCC staff support media reports. Most men not only gained much needed weight but also came away with marketable job skills and a better education. According to the national CCC director, approximately 87 percent of CCC enrollees took advantage of camp education and training opportunities.[7] Those willing to put forth the effort overcame illiteracy, while others went on to secure a high school diploma. Such opportunities were afforded several men from Camp Hawthorne, including Vernard "Bud" Wilbur who completed his high school education while stationed in the CCC:

> Mr. Pope . . . from the Sacramento area . . . noticed that I dropped out of school my senior year. . . . I think there was about four or five of us . . . who were given the opportunity to go to Hawthorne High School with the local kids, and I did. We went to school eight hours a day and I finished and got my high school equivalency diploma from the State of New York that way. . . . In fact, when I joined the Army Air Corp in 1941 and went into my basic training, most of the commanding officers would ask people, "Were you ever in the Civilian Conservation Corps, and how long were [you] in, and what was your discipline like?" And, normally those men were given a better job and a better chance for a promotion to private first class.[8]

The on-the-job training also improved the future earning potential of most enrollees. As the economic picture improved in the late 1930s, jobs were available to those with skills. A Bureau of Reclamation supervising engineer proudly cited the variety of positions available to skilled enrollees: one enrollee who served as a warehouse and tool-room clerk in Montana earned ninety dollars a month as a stockroom clerk in an automobile agency, a carpenter's assistant in Nevada earned five dollars per day working as a rough carpenter for a silver mine, a CCC truck driver in Oregon accepted a truck-driving position for an oil company in his home state of Kentucky for three dollars per day, and a CCC tractor operator earned four dollars a day working on an Idaho farm.[9]

Enrollees assigned to camp administration and support also found jobs. Camp Carson River cook Michael DeCarlo's culinary training provided lifelong benefits:

> We all went back to Ft. Dix, New Jersey . . . and then we got our discharge from there . . . and on there it said I was a second cook. Later on when I was twenty-two or twenty-three years old, the war broke out so I went to join the Merchant

To support the war effort, full-time automotive and radio schools were established at camps around the state. Shown is Camp Boulder City enrollee Mike Sitka, at work in the radio room, ca. 1940. Courtesy Boulder City Museum and Historical Society (Burns Collection)

> Marines in New York City. I went down to what you call the War Ship Administration, and when I told them I wanted to join, I showed them my [CCC] discharge.
>
> "You were a cook?"
>
> I didn't know they were desperate for cooks, and I got in right away. A couple days later I was on a ship as a cook. That's how I got in the Merchant Marines.[10]

By joining the CCC, the men embarked on a grand adventure. During the darkest days of the Depression, the men were provided opportunities available to only a select group of Americans. Army officers and supervisors also benefited. Regular and reserve officers received training in command techniques, and foremen earned a respectable wage supervising field projects. An estimated 7,079 Nevada residents participated in the program in various capacities. The CCC program helped them through tough times following mine and mill closures and rock-bottom livestock prices. Nearly 24,000 other men were sent to Nevada from the heartland or east of the Mississippi.[11] Nevada seemed foreign to many of the men, and working conditions were not always easy. President Roosevelt's wish for a "pleasant . . . stay in the woods" may have been appropriate for those assigned to the eastern seaboard or the Pacific Northwest. In Nevada, the men usually worked in a treeless environment and in extreme temperatures. The intensely hot summers of southern Nevada were a constant health hazard, and the freezing winters of northern Nevada often stranded men in camp for days or weeks. Still, deserters were rare until late in the CCC program when more lucrative jobs became available.

Despite the CCC's male focus, the lives of many females were touched by the CCC program. One unsung female hero, Edna Timmons, deserves recognition for her strength and stamina. A native of Midas, Edna was the wife of Wilbur Timmons, a dedicated foreman at Camp Paradise. She summed up her CCC experience as a "real challenge."[12] She raised two young children while traveling with her husband to various projects, all the while living in a one-room portable trailer that was home. Edna Timmons was a friendly face to many homesick boys whom her husband trained.

The couple's mettle was tested as a result of a devastating fire that took the lives of five Camp Paradise enrollees on July 28, 1939. At least five hundred local men and northern Nevada enrollees fought the eight thousand–acre brush fire in the Santa Rosa Range near Orovada on that fateful day. When Wilbur Timmons led his crew of twenty-three CCC firefighters up a

Edna and Wilbur Timmons *(on right)* pose with other Camp Paradise employees in front of their portable homes. Courtesy Edna Timmons

slope, the wind shifted and a back draft engulfed five enrollees in a ring of flames. The stricken men—four from New York and one from Kansas—ranged in age from eighteen to twenty-two.[13] Although a full-scale investigation exonerated Timmons, the incident took its toll on his family.

The tragedy sent shock waves across the West. Federal agencies and CCC officials were forced to reexamine their safety practices, training protocol, and raise the minimum age of CCC firefighters. The Forest Service erected a rock monument honoring their fallen comrades on the side of U.S. Highway 95, a few miles from the scene of the accident. CCC foreman and master stonemason Virgil Pascuale supervised the rock work.[14] As of this writing, the memorial is the only monument to CCC workers in Nevada.

The Orovada fire was undoubtedly the worst tragedy suffered by the CCC program in Nevada. For the most part, government and army officials ran their operations as safely as possible, and relatively few CCC workers lost their lives, on or off duty. Forestry officials maintained that the number of accidents were no higher than average civilian industrial rates.[15] Nonetheless, scores of CCC enrollees and staff never returned home. Their deaths

The smoke had barely cleared when air crews began to search for five missing Camp Paradise firefighters. Tragically, none of the men was found alive. The Orovada fire struck a devastating blow to the CCC program in Nevada. Courtesy Edmund Rosowski

were usually the result of illness or vehicle accidents. However, weather also played a role. A wicked winter storm in 1937 killed a nineteen-year-old Kentuckian and his foreman outside of Eureka. The two men froze to death in thirty-five-below-zero temperatures after leaving their stalled vehicle in search of help.[16]

During pilgrimages to Nevada, former enrollees occasionally wander into local museums, park offices, and ranger stations in hopes of finding the camps where they came of age. Many CCC alumni return with their families to share their memories of a championship tournament, hard work in the heat and cold, the soda shop, or theater in town. Others try to look up old friends or their families. Although Nevada's alumni are a small group by comparison to larger states, at least two gatherings of Nevada enrollees

---

Opposite page. The Forest Service and Camp Paradise staff erected this monument to honor the deceased enrollees. A roadside rest stop was later built around the memorial on U.S. Route 95. Courtesy Bureau of Land Management, Winnemucca Field Office

FRANK W. BARKER GEORGE J. KENNEDY
WALTER JAMES EARNEST R. TIPPIN
FRANK J. VITALE
MEMBERS OF THE
CIVILIAN CONSERVATION CORPS
COMPANY 1212
PARADISE CAMP F-5
WHO GAVE THEIR LIVES FOR THE
CONSERVATION OF NEVADA'S NATURAL
RESOURCES, WHILE FIGHTING FIRE
ABOUT THREE MILES EAST OF THIS
POINT ON JULY 28, 1939
THIS MARKER DONATED AND ERECTED BY THE
ENROLLEES, THEIR OFFICERS AND FOREMEN OF
THE U.S. FOREST SERVICE C.C.C. CAMPS OF
REGION NO. 4

have taken place. The U.S. Forest Service hosted a reunion at the Paradise Valley Guard Station north of Winnemucca in August 1990, and a tristate reunion for California, Nevada, and Oregon alumni was held around the same time at Tule Lake in northern California.[17]

Guest registers at the Lost City Museum and Fort Churchill State Park Visitors' Center attest to frequent visits through the mid-1990s. Since then, the numbers have dwindled.

CCC alumni chapters around the country continue to sponsor yearly events to stimulate public awareness. Recently, the consolidated efforts of CCC alumni successfully stimulated national attention for this bygone program. Senate Resolution 207, designating March 31, 2002, as "National Civilian Conservation Corps Day," pays homage to the three million men who contributed to the restoration of America's natural resources.[18]

Although the CCC was never revived, subsequent programs such as the Job Corps and the California and Nevada Conservation Corps have modeled their youth programs after CCC principles. Although the Great Depression is long over, new sets of social and economic problems afflict factions of today's youth. Given the opportunity, CCC alumni are happy to share their experiences with their young counterparts. Beneath their warm, grandfatherly demeanor, the message is usually to the point: *You can do it. Hard work and perseverance paid off for our generation. The CCC kept us off the streets. We are proud of what we did for our country, our families, and for future generations of Americans.*

APPENDIX

Compilation of Nevada CCC Camps and Their Supervisory Agencies

Division of Grazing/Grazing Service CCC Camps

Public Domain Grazing (DG) (G)

Project No.	*Company No.*	*Camp Name*	*Nearest Post Office*	*Dates of Operation*
DG-7	1907	Swinford Springs (Vya) (in Nevada)	Cedarville, CA	5-18-35/10-24-35
"	590	"	"	5-13-36/10-31-36
"	3876	"	"	5-7-37/10-1-37
DG/G-16	537	Sunnyside	Ely	10-26-35/4-30-36
"	3236	"	"	4-30-36/5-24-36
"	4790	"	"	10-20-36/4-20-39
"	3542	"	"	4-21-39–7-7-41
DG/G-17	2534	Pershing	Oreana/Lovelock	10-26-35/10-9-37
"	225	"	"	10-10-37/10-23-38
DG-18	2501	Mill Creek	Battle Mountain	10-25-35/4-14-36
"	3237	"	"	4-15-36/5-2-37
DG/G-19	4292	Delmues	Pioche	6-20-35/7-20-35
"	1257	"	"	8-20-35/10-24-35

Division of Grazing/Grazing Service CCC Camps (cont'd)

Public Domain Grazing (DG) (G)

Project No.	*Company No.*	*Camp Name*	*Nearest Post Office*	*Dates of Operation*
"	590	"	"	5-5-37/10-10-37
"	4428	"	"	10-11-37/6-22-38
"	2597	"	"	10-21-38/11-30-41
"	3805	"	"	12-1-41/6-30-42
DG-20	1504	Sadlers Ranch	Eureka	10-26-35/5-31-37
DG/G-21	2532	Indian Springs	Ely	10-22-35/5-9-41
"	5435	"	"	5-10-41/7-7-41
"	3542	"	"	7-8-41/5-31-42
DG/G-22	4291	Muddy River	Moapa	6-30-35/7-20-35
"	1290	"	"	8-20-35/9-30-35
"	736	"	"	10-1-35/5-31-36
"	590	"	"	11-1-36/5-4-37
"	4419	"	"	10-13-37/10-20-38
"	3532	"	"	10-21-38/6-30-40
"	6434	"	"	10-16-40/8-31-41
DG-64	3237	Lamoille	Lamoille	5-3-37/10-14-37
DG-67	3237	Fort Churchill	Weeks/Fernley	10-15-37/8-28-38

Division of Grazing/Grazing Service CCC Camps (cont'd)

Public Domain Grazing (DG) (G)

Project No.	*Company No.*	*Camp Name*	*Nearest Post Office*	*Dates of Operation*
DG/G-82	4428	Warm Creek	Wells	6-23-38/11-30-41
DG/G-83	4601	Tuscarora	Tuscarora	9-9-38/10-24-38
"	4429	"	"	5-2-39/9-30-39
"	6434	"	"	7-10-40/10-15-40
DG/G-85	1216	Quinn River	Winnemucca	10-20-38/1-19-41
"	6458	"	"	1-20-41/11-5-41
DG/G-86	5476	Gerlach	Gerlach	10-24-38/11-30-41
DG/G-87	3237	Minden	Gardnerville and Minden	8-29-38/7-6-41
DG/G-108	1685	Hubbard Ranch	Wells	8-21-38/1-22-41
"	5726	"	"	1-23-41/8-21-41
"	2539	"	"	8-22-41/7-28-42
DG/G-118	4601	Twin Bridges	Elko	10-25-38/1-25-41
"	5725	"	"	1-26-41/8-21-41
"	2529	"	"	8-22-41/11-30-41
DG/G-119	3273	Hawthorne #1	Hawthorne	7-23-39/5-16-41
"	6457	"	"	5-17-41/7-6-41
DG/G-120	1625	Golconda	Golconda and Winnemucca	10-18-38/1-16-41

Division of Grazing/Grazing Service CCC Camps (cont'd)

Public Domain Grazing (DG) (G)

Project No.	*Company No.*	*Camp Name*	*Nearest Post Office*	*Dates of Operation*
"	6453	"	"	1-17-41/5-31-41
"	6458	"	"	11-6-41/11-30-41
DG/G-121	1706	Cherry Creek	Cherry Creek	10-11-38/4-22-39
"	5435	"	"	4-23-39/5-9-41
DG/G-122	3542	Las Vegas	Las Vegas	11-28-38/4-20-39
"	2557	"	"	10-5-39/7-4-41
DG/G-124	1915	Westgate	Fallon	10-20-38/7-31-41
DG/G-128	3566	Mason Valley	Mason	9-29-38/7-9-40
"	5497	"	"	7-10-40/5-31-42
DG/G-129	225	Lovelock	Lovelock	10-24-38/1-26-41
"	6461	"	"	1-27-41/7-31-41
G-180	3237	Truckee Meadows	Reno	7-7-41/11-3-41
"	6458	"	"	12-1-41/12-31-41

Bureau of Reclamation CCC Camps

Bureau of Reclamation (BR)

BR-34	2501	Newlands	Fallon	6-13-35/7-20-35
"	295	"	"	11-4-35/1-16-36
"	4743	"	"	1-17-36/7-31-37

Bureau of Reclamation CCC Camps (cont'd)

Bureau of Reclamation (BR)

Project No.	*Company No.*	*Camp Name*	*Nearest Post Office*	*Dates of Operation*
BR-34	3206	"	"	10-11-37/5-31-40
"	3206	"	"	10-12-40/4-30-41
"	5495	"	"	12-1-41/4-30-42
BR-35	2505	Carson River	Fallon	6-13-35/7-20-35
"	2533	"	"	10-21-35/10-9-37
"	1225	"	"	10-10-37/4-30-39
"	1225	"	"	10-5-39/11-5-41
BR-36	4235	Lovelock	Lovelock	6-13-35/7-20-35
"	1216	"	"	8-20-35/10-19-38
BR-37	4236	Reno	Reno	6-13-35/7-20-35
"	258	"	"	11-11-35/8-2-38
BR-52	4237	Walker River (or Topaz Lake)	Wellington	6-13-35/7-20-35
"	295*	"	"	11-4-35/1-16-36

U. S. Biological Survey/Fish and Wildlife Service CCC Camps

Fish and Wildlife Service (FWS, formerly the Bureau of Fisheries [BF] or Biological Survey [BS])

BF-1	994	Board Corrals (camp in Nevada)	Cedarville, CA	5-18-35/10-15-35
"	737	"	"	5-6-36/10-24-36

*Operated as joint camp with BR-34. Camp was seasonal during the summers of 1936, 1937, and possibly 1938.

U. S. Biological Survey/Fish and Wildlife Service CCC Camps (cont'd)

Fish and Wildlife Service (FWS, formerly the Bureau of Fisheries [BF] or Biological Survey [BS])

Project No.	*Company No.*	*Camp Name*	*Nearest Post Office*	*Dates of Operation*
"	3883	"	"	4-30-37/10-31-37
BF-2 ; later BS-2 and FWS-2	1915	Charles Sheldon	Winnemucca	7-?-38/10-?-38
"	5460	"	"	5-18-39/8-28-41
BS-3; later FWS-3	3691	Ruby Lake	Wells	8-8-40/1-22-41
"	5724	"	"	1-23-41/8-23-41
"	2557	"	"	8-24-41/5-31-42
FWS-4	2557	Corn Creek, a.k.a. Corn Creek Ranch	Las Vegas	7-5-41/8-23-41?

National Park Service and Nevada State Parks System CCC Camps

State Park Service (SP); National Park Service (NP)

NP-1/SP-1	974	Overton	Overton	10-15-33/5-1-34
"	573	"	"	11-3-34/1-14-36
SP-3/NP-3	974	Cathedral Gorge	Panaca	10-1-34/5-2-35
SP-4/NP-4	573	Boulder City; Later, Boulder City #1	Boulder City	1-15-36/3-31-37 4-1-37/11-30-41
SP-5/NP-5	590	Fort Churchill, a.k.a. Big Bend	Weeks, Fernley, and Churchill	5-15-35/3-31-35
SP-6/NP-6	2536	Boulder City #2	Boulder City	10-26-35/3-31-37
"	"	"	"	4-1-37/3-31-42
NP-7	2536	Boulder City (merger of #1 & #2)	Boulder City	4-1-42/7-28-42

U.S. Navy CCC Camps in Hawthorne

Project No.	*Company No.*	*Camp Name*	*Nearest Post Office*	*Dates of Operation*
M-1/N-1 (later Navy 1)	1348/1915	Hawthorne #1	Hawthorne	10-27-33/11-26-33 11-27-33/10-19-38
M-2 (later Navy 2)	4238 260	Hawthorne #2	Hawthorne	6-20-35/7-20-35 7-24-35/1-16-36
"	4740	"	"	1-17-36/10-14-36

National Forest CCC Camps

Forest Service (F)

F-1	973	Lamoille	Lamoille	5-22-33/11-13-33
"	"	"	Elko	4-25-34/11-11-34
"	"	"	"	5-10-35/10-31-35
"	2512	"	"	6-3-36/10-31-36
"	1212	"	"	5-10-40/7-18-40
	6433	"	"	7-19-40/10-24-40
F-2	1348*	Paradise (Site #1)	Paradise Valley	5-27-33/10-26-33
F-3	1915	Berry Creek	McGill	5-29-33/11-6-33
F-4	974	Charleston Mountain (or Kyle Canyon)	Las Vegas	5-10-33/10-14-33
"	538	"	"	4-24-34/10-31-34
"	2537	"	"	5-24-36/11-11-36
"	"	"	"	6-5-37/10-31-37
"	5441	"	"	5-10-38/10-16-38

National Forest CCC Camps (cont'd)

Forest Service (F)

Project No.	*Company No.*	*Camp Name*	*Nearest Post Office*	*Dates of Operation*
"	"	"	"	5-5-39/10-7-39
"	1530	"	"	5-10-40/10-25-40
"	"	"	"	5-10-41/10-31-41
"	"	"	"	5-15-42/7-28-42
F-5	973	Paradise (Site #2)	Paradise Valley	11-12-34/5-9-35
"	230	"	"	7-24-35/1-16-36
"	4706	"	"	1-17-36/10-12-37
"	1212	"	"	10-13-37/5-9-40
"	6433	"	"	10-25-40/6-13-41
F-6	?	Galena	Galena	? ca. 1940
F-7	2512	Reese River	Austin	9-12-35/6-2-36
"	"	"	"	11-1-36/5-31-37
"	6433	"	"	6-14-41/5-31-42

*Company 1348 redesignated Company 1915 following transfer from Camp Paradise (F-2) to Camp Hawthorne (M-1)

Soil Conservation Service Camps

SCS/Private Land Erosion (PE)

Project No.	*Company No.*	*Camp Name*	*Nearest Post Office*	*Dates of Operation*
SCS-1/or PE-202	1915	Moapa	Moapa	11-7-33/11-26-33
"	536	"	"	10-16-34/6-1-35
SCS-2/or PE 203	973	Caliente	Hiko	11-14-33/4-24-34
SCS-3 (formerly PE-204)	2513	Panaca	Panaca	9-13-35/6-30-41
"	880	"	"	12-1-41/7-14-42
SCS-4 (formerly PE-205)	2538	Bunkerville (Virgin Valley)	Bunkerville	10-23-35/5-31-36
"	4791	"	"	10-19-36/5-31-37
SCS-5	3258	Pioche	Pioche	6-28-36/10-31-36
SCS-6 (formerly G-87)	6457	Minden	Minden	7-7-41/10-31-41
Private Erosion Control/Private Entity (PE) (P)				
PE-204	974	Panaca	Panaca	5-2-34/9-30-34
PE-205	537	Bunkerville (Virgin Valley)	Bunkerville	10-16-34/5-31-35
PE-206 *(P-206 as of 10-1-35)	538	Wells Siding	Logandale	11-1-34/6-29-35
"	2537	"	"	10-23-35/5-23-36 11-12-36/6-4-37
"	5441	"	"	10-11-37/5-9-38 10-17-37/5-4-39
"	1530	"	"	10-8-39/5-9-40 10-26-40/5-9-41 11-1-41/5-14-42

*Private forest

NOTES

Introduction

1. James W. Hulse, *Forty Years in the Wilderness: Impressions of Nevada, 1940–1980;* Michael S. Green and Gary E. Elliott, "Gaming and Tourism," 167–68.

2. Leonard Arrington, "The New Deal in the West: A Preliminary Statistical Inquiry"; J. J. Wallis, "The Political Economy of New Deal Spending Revisited, Again: With and Without Nevada," 157.

3. Eugene P. Moehring, "The Federal Trigger," 209.

4. Wallis, "Political Economy," 140–70; Arrington, "New Deal in the West," 315–16.

5. "Directory of the Civilian Conservation Corps Camps, Tenth Period, 1937–1938."

6. Jim F. Couch and William F. Shughart II, *The Political Economy of the New Deal,* 114–15.

7. Donald Dale Jackson, "They Were Poor, Hungry, and They Built to Last," 68. A separate CCC program was administered on reservations by the Office of Indian Affairs (now the Bureau of Indian Affairs). Because of major differences in administration and eligibility requirements, the Civilian Conservation Corps–Indian Division (called CCC-ID) will be addressed elsewhere.

8. Per Harold Truman Smith's dissertation, "New Deal Relief Programs in Nevada, 1933 to 1935" (from NARA records).

9. Marion Wilbur, personal conversation with Renée Corona Kolvet, June 20, 2004.

10. "Roosevelt's Tree Army: A Brief History of the Civilian Conservation Corps."

1 | A Nation Brought to Its Knees

1. Ralph Hash, interview by Victoria Ford, October 25, 2000, University of Nevada Oral History Program, Reno; *New York Times,* April 16, 1935.

2. Frank Freidel, *Franklin D. Roosevelt: A Rendezvous with Destiny,* 62.

3. Don C. Reading, "A Statistical Analysis of New Deal Economic Programs in the Forty-eight States," 7.

4. David M. Kennedy, *Freedom from Fear: The American People in Depression and War, 1929–1945,* 135–40.

5. Ibid., 135, 145.

6. "Memorandum for the Press," released January 2, 1938, Civilian Conservation Corps, NARA, Record Group 35, entry 66, Press Releases, National Archives, College Park, Md.

7. John A. Salmond, *The Civilian Conservation Corps, 1933–1942: A New Deal Case Study,* 4.

8. Joseph Ruchty, interview by Victoria Ford, June 22, 2000, University of Nevada Oral History Program, Reno.

9. Salmond, *Civilian Conservation Corps,* 36.

10. Harry Dallas, "An Army for Land Conservation Work."

11. Frank Freidel, *Franklin D. Roosevelt: Launching the New Deal,* 263.

12. Hash interview.

13, Salmond, *Civilian Conservation Corps,* 41.

14. W. Frank Persons to Frances Perkins, May 2, 1933, Official File 268, Civilian Conservation Corps, Franklin D. Roosevelt Library, National Archives, Hyde Park, N.Y. (hereafter cited as FDR Library).

15. Salmond, *Civilian Conservation Corps,* 40.

16. George Dern to Franklin D. Roosevelt, June 30, 1933, Official File 268, Civilian Conservation Corps, FDR Library.

17. Ruchty interview.

18. FDR's White House address in *Happy Days* (July 10, 1933).

19. Jackson, "They Were Poor," 66–77.

20. Kennedy, *Freedom from Fear,* 783.

2 | Nevada Fights Back

1. Jerome Edwards, "Nevada Power Broker: Pat McCarran and His Political Machine?" 98.

2. *Fallon Standard,* August 17, 1938.

3. Jerome Edwards, *Pat McCarran: Political Boss of Nevada,* 77–78.

4. Marshall Crawford, interview by Victoria Ford, November 6, 2000, University of Nevada Oral History Program, Reno.

5. Richard Lowitt and Maurine Beasley, eds., *One-third of a Nation: Lorena Hickok Reports on the Great Depression,* 317.

6. *Reno Evening Gazette,* June 12, 1935.

7. Russell R. Elliott, *Growing Up in a Company Town,* 135–38.

8. Betty Glad, *Key Pittman: The Tragedy of a Senate Insider,* 218.

9. Russell R. Elliott, *History of Nevada,* 139.

10. Ibid., 297.

11. Edwards, *Pat McCarran,* 50, 289.

12. Larry Schweikart, "A New Perspective on George Wingfield and Nevada Banking, 1920–1933," 331.

13. C. Elizabeth Raymond, *George Wingfield: Owner and Operator of Nevada,* 210–19.

14. *Carson City Appeal,* April 9, 1937.

15. Smith, "New Deal Relief Programs," iv.

16. *Reno Evening Gazette,* February 9, 1934; Edwards, *Pat McCarran,* 69.

17. Bruce Bustard, *A New Deal for the Arts,* 1-3.

18. *Reno Evening Gazette,* January 3, 1938.

19. Lowitt and Beasley, *One-third of a Nation,* xxiii.

20. Ibid., 317.

21. Ruchty interview.

22. *Nevada State Journal,* September 20, 1933.

23. *Carson City Appeal,* June 8, 1938.

24. Hash interview.

25. *Carson City Appeal,* July 13, 1938.

26. Robert Fechner to Franklin D. Roosevelt, December 10, 1937, Official File 268, Civilian Conservation Corps, FDR Library.

27. Alison T. Otis and others, "The Forest Service and the Civilian Conservation Corps, 1933–1942."

28. Tim Pruitt, "Cricket Gangs," 114–16.

29. *Elko Independent,* April 16, 1937.

30. James Muhn and Hanson R. Stuart, *Opportunity and Challenge: The Story of the BLM,* 37–41.

31. Vernard (Bud) Wilbur, interview by Victoria Ford, July 19, 2000, University of Nevada Oral History Program, Reno.

32. *Nevada State Journal,* August 30, 1933.

33. *Nevada State Parks System Plan,* 1–6.

3 | The CCC Program in Nevada

1. Hash interview.

2. *Camp Newlands Courier,* 1936.

3. Renée Corona Kolvet, "A New Deal in the Desert: Civilian Conservation Corps in Nevada, Mapping Project."

4. *Ely Daily Times,* January, 14, 1937.

5. "Instructions Governing the Selection of Veterans to Compose the Veterans Contingent of the Civilian Conservation Corps, Supplement no. 2 to Instructions of September 7, 1937."

6. "A Brief Summary of Certain Phases of the Civilian Conservation Corps, Ne-

vada, April 1933–June 30, 1938"; "Monthly Statistical Summaries for July and September 1941"; Wilbur Timmons, interview by Peggy McGuckian, June 29, 1984, Collection of the BLM, Winnemucca Field Office.

7. "Brief Summary, April 1933–June 30, 1938."

8. "Statement of Robert Fechner to the U.S. Senate Special Committee to Investigate Unemployment, March 15, 1938"; DOL, "Summary of CCC Statistical Data for Nevada, July 22, 1939."

9. "Monthly Statistical Summary for July through September 1941"; "A Brief Summary of Certain Phases of the Civilian Conservation Corps (Alaska through Wyoming and the United States), 1942."

10. "Pictorial Review of Company 1212, Camp Paradise."

11. W. Frank Persons, "Selecting 1,800,000 Young Men for the C.C.C."

12. Gilbert Ross to W. Frank Persons, August 19, 1936, NARA, CCC, Record Group 35, entry 43, General Letters, 1937–1939, Nevada.

13. *Reno Evening Gazette,* June 15, 1935.

14. C. J. Thornton, *Entrepreneur: Agriculture, Business, Politics; An Oral History Conducted by Mary Ellen Glass,* 118.

15. Herman Haynes, interview by Victoria Ford, October 6, 2000, University of Nevada Oral History Program, Reno.

16. *Las Vegas Evening Review Journal,* May 11, 1933.

17. *Las Vegas Evening Review Journal,* July 3, 1933.

18. Crawford interview.

19. Hash interview.

20. DOL, "Summary of CCC Statistical Data, Nevada, January 6, 1939."

21. *Your CCC: A Handbook for Enrollees,* 53; Olen Cole Jr., *The African-American Experience in the Civilian Conservation Corps,* 28.

22. "Memorandum for the Press," December 5, 1935, NARA, CCC, Record Group 35, entry 66, Press Releases, Nevada.

23. DOL, "Age Distribution of 238,846 Juniors Selected and Accepted for the Civilian Conservation Corps, October 1–November 15, 1935, April 1–15, 1936, and July 1–31, 1936"; DOL, "Age Distribution of Juniors Enrolled in the Civilian Conservation Corps during the June–August Enrollment, 1935."

24. "Statement of Robert Fechner"; DOL, "Height of Juniors Accepted for Enrollment, January 1940; Weight of Juniors Accepted for Enrollment, January 1940."

25. DOL, "Fiscal Year Report for CCC Activities for Year Ended June 30, 1937"; "Years of Schooling Completed by Junior Enrollees in January 1940 and October 1940."

26. "Urban-Rural Classifications of Juniors Accepted for Enrollment in the Civilian Conservation Corps, January, 1941."

4 | Outsiders and Small-Town Folk

1. *Mineral County Independent,* October 11, 1933.

2. Calvin Cushing, interview by Renée Corona Kolvet, April 20, 2000, University of Nevada Oral History Program, Reno.

3. *Reno Evening Gazette,* May 22, 1935.

4. *Reno Evening Gazette,* June 6, 1935.

5. *Mineral County Independent,* December 27, 1933; *Reno Evening Gazette,* June 4, 1935.

6. A. W. Stockmen to J. J. McEntee, "Special Report no. 138," December 9, 1938, NARA, CCC Record Group 35, entry 115, Camp Inspection Reports, Nevada, Camp Reno.

7. Cushing interview.

8. *Reno Evening Gazette,* December 23, 1935.

9. Vernard "Bud" Wilbur, "Highlights of My CCC Camp Days," n.d., on file at the National Association of Civilian Conservation Corps Alumni, St. Louis, Mo.

10. Jane Pieplow, "Government Programs Come to Fallon and Churchill County, Civilian Conservation Corps."

11. *Fallon Standard,* June 21, 1939.

12. Andrew "Andy" Jackson, interview by Peggy McGuckian, April 24, 1984, Collection of the BLM, Winnemucca Field Office.

13. Timmons interview.

14. Smith, "New Deal Relief Programs," 112–25.

15. Rex J. Hines, interview by Victoria Ford, August 28, 2000, Collection of the University of Nevada Oral History Program, Reno.

16. John "Jack" Wurst, letters to Renée Corona Kolvet, June 16, August 5, 2000.

17. William "W. D." Ferguson, interview by Victoria Ford, October 4, 2000, Collection of the University of Nevada Oral History Program, Reno.

18. Archie Murchie, *The Free Life of a Ranger, 1929–1965,* 335.

19. Elmer Randall, interview by Victoria Ford, July 6, 2000, Collection of the University of Nevada Oral History Program, Reno.

20. *Eureka Sentinel,* April 3, 1937.

21. *Ely Daily Times,* December 19, 1935.

22. *Eureka Sentinel,* January 11, 1936; *Mineral County Independent,* July 20, 1934.

23. Crawford interview.

24. Edna Timmons, interview by Dan Bennett, October 12, 2000, University of Nevada Oral History Program, Reno.

25. *Mineral County Independent,* October 3, 1934.

26. Peggy McGuckian, "Report Commemorating 50 Years of the Taylor Grazing Act, Bureau of Land Management," Winnemucca Field Office.

27. Gus Bartley, telephone conversation with Renée Corona Kolvet, June 15, 2001; Dixie (Hendricks) Whipple, conversation with Renée Corona Kolvet, July 12, 2001.

28. E. S. Adams to the director of the Civilian Conservation Corps, November 21, 1939, NARA, CCC, Record Group 35, entry 115, Camp Inspection Reports, Nevada, Camp BS-2.

29. Ralph Hash, conversation with Renée Corona Kolvet, July 5, 2001.

30. Cushing interview.

31. *Reno Evening Gazette,* August 10, 1936.

32. *Reno Evening Gazette,* September 3, 1936.

33. *Ely Daily Times,* June 9, 1936; *Ely Daily Times,* June 28, 1937.

34. *Ely Daily Times,* September 12, 1936; *Ely Daily Times,* November 10, 1936; *Mineral County Independent,* December 27, 1933.

35. Wilbur interview.

36. Terese Thomas, interview by Dennis McBride, May 19, 1995, Boulder City Oral History Project, Boulder City (Nev.) Library.

37. *Nevada State Journal,* February 28, 1940.

5 | Rehabilitating the Public Domain: The Grazing Service CCC Program

1. *Eureka Sentinel,* December 21, 1935.

2. Ibid.

3. *Nevada State Journal,* April 26, 1941.

4. *Reno Evening Gazette,* October 31, 1938.

5. *Las Vegas Evening Review Journal,* June 15, 1942.

6. Muhn and Stuart, *Opportunity and Challenge,* 37–41.

7. Derrel S. Fulwider, "From Resource Management to People Management: Reflections of a Federal Land Manager."

8. *Ely Daily Times,* February 26, 1936.

9. *Eureka Sentinel,* March 27, 1937.

10. Paul Herndon, *The Taylor Grazing Act: History of Grazing on Public Lands,* 75.

11. *Eureka Sentinel,* June 13, 1936.

12. Edward T. Taylor, "American Democracy on the Range."

13. Pat McCarran to Thomas Woodnut Miller, June 30, 1938, Thomas Woodnut Miller Papers.

14. Wilbur interview.

15. *Nevada State Journal,* April 5, 1939.

16. A. W. Stockman to the director of the Civilian Conservation Corps, Supplemental for Special Detachment, G-87, Co. 3237, October 31, 1939, NARA, FSA, CCC, Record Group 35, entry 115, Camp Inspection Reports, Nevada, Camp Minden.

17. F. Sommer Schmidt, "Trail Building as a Means of Affecting Range Conservation and Management," in Miller Papers.

18. Marla Griswold, conversation with Renée Corona Kolvet, April 11, 2000.

19. *Reno Gazette Journal,* June 8, 1974.

20. "Project Application, Project no. 525, Camp 87, Region 3."

21. *Record Courier,* August 9, 1940.

22. *Reno Evening Gazette,* August 10, 1936.

23. *Tonopah Daily Times,* April 14, 1941.

24. *Reno Evening Gazette,* August 2, 1936.

25. *Nevada State Journal,* July 15, 1941.

26. *Nevada State Journal,* June 18, 1941.

27. *Reno Evening Gazette,* April 26, 1942.

28. Patrick McCarran to L. R. Brooks, July 14, 1941, Patrick McCarran Papers; McCarran to Brooks, July 19, 1941, ibid.

29. James McEntee, "Memorandum for the Press," August 17, 1941, NARA, FSA, CCC, Record Group 35, entry 66, Press Releases, Nevada.

30. *Humboldt Star,* February 17, 1941.

31. *Ely Daily Times,* December 16, 1941.

32. Claude A. Chadwell, interview by Victoria Ford, November 10, 2000, University of Nevada Oral History Program, Reno.

6 | Irrigating the Desert West: The Bureau of Reclamation's CCC Program

1. *Reno Evening Gazette,* July 27, 1933.

2. John M. Townley, *Turn This Water into Gold: The Story of the Newlands Project,* 23, 69.

3. *Fallon Standard,* December 19, 1934.

4. Christine Pfaff, "The Bureau of Reclamation and the Civilian Conservation Corps, 1933–1942."

5. Toni Rae Linenberger, *Dams, Dynamos, and Development: The Bureau of Reclamation's Power Program and Electrification of the West.*

6. Townley, *Turn This Water into Gold.*

7. Ruchty interview.

8. Harry Norman, interview by Victoria Ford, October 3, 2000, University of Nevada Oral History Program, Reno.

9. Pfaff, "Bureau of Reclamation."

10. J. R. Alcorn, "Life History Notes on the Piute Ground Squirrel."

11. Margaret (Peggy) Hatton Wheat became a respected expert on the Stillwater Paiute peoples. She helped Ralph Hash find a job at Nevada Auto Supply in Reno in 1937.

12. Hash interview.

13. *Annual Project History, Humboldt Project, 1934, 1935, 1936.*

14. Thomas Williamson, "CCC Construction of Parapet and Curb Walls Rye Patch Dam, Humboldt Project, Nevada," 15, 16.

15. *Reno Evening Gazette,* July 20, 1935.

16. *Fallon Standard,* December 19, 1934.

17. Pfaff, "Bureau of Reclamation," 135.

18. "CCC Boys at Boca Dam Forced to 'Scab' by the Bureau of Reclamation," Washoe County Water Conservation District, Correspondence, NC379, box 1, file 33, Nevada Historical Society, Reno.

19. A. W. Stockmen to J. J. McEntee, "Special Report no. 138," NARA, CCC, Record Group 115, Camp Inspection Reports, Nevada, Camp Reno.

20. *Reno Evening Gazette,* November 30, 1936.

21. *Reno Evening Gazette,* February 7, 1941; *Record Courier,* February 14, 1941.

7 | Developing National Wildlife Refuges: The Fish and Wildlife Service Program

1. "Short History of the Refuge System, Organization and Growth (1921–1955)," http://www.refuge.fws.gov.

2. *Record Courier,* April 8, 1938.

3. Ibid.

4. A. W. Stockman to J. J. McEntee, May 9, 1938, NARA, Record Group 35, entry 115, Camp Inspection Reports, Nevada, Camp Charles Sheldon.

5. M. J. Bowen to the director of the Civilian Conservation Corps, November 19, 1940, Record Group 35, entry 115, Camp Inspection Reports, Nevada, Camp Charles Sheldon.

6. Ibid.

7. Ralph Murphy, "Sheldon National Wildlife Refuge: A Collection of Historical Vignettes."

8. Lou Ann Speulda, "Evaluation and Assessment Report for the Virgin Valley Campground Bath House, Sheldon NWR, Humboldt County, Nevada."

9. *Mineral County Independent,* July 13, 1938.

10. A. W. Stockman to the director of the Civilian Conservation Corps, Supplemental Report, October 30, 1939, Record Group 35, entry 115, Camp Inspection Reports, Nevada, Camp Charles Sheldon.

11. M. J. Bowen to the director of the Civilian Conservation Corps, November 19, 1940, ibid.

12. Speulda, "Evaluation and Assessment Report."

13. "Quarterly Narrative Report, May 8 through June 30, 1940, Ruby Lake Camp FWS-3, Wells, Nevada."

14. Camp Inspection Report, December 11, 1940, Camp Ruby FWS-3.

15. "Quarterly Narrative Report, May 8 through June 30, 1940."

16. "Quarterly Narrative Report, July through September, 1940, Ruby Lake Camp FWS-3, Wells, Nevada."

17. "Quarterly Narrative Report for the Months of October, November, Decem-

ber, 1941 and January, February, March and April, 1942 to May 15, 1942, Ruby Lake Camp FWS-3, Wells, Nevada."

18. "Quarterly Narrative Report for Months of July, August and September [1941], Ruby Lake Camp FWS-3, Wells, Nevada."

19. "Quarterly Narrative Report for the Months of October, November, December, 1941 and January, February, March and April, 1942 to May 15, 1942."

20. Ibid.

21. Haynes interview.

22. *Desert National Wildlife Range.*

23. Bruce Zeller, conversation with Renée Corona Kolvet, September 12, 2000; *Fallon Standard,* March 20, 1940.

24. *Nevada State Journal,* July 26, 1940; *Las Vegas Evening Review Journal,* October 3, 1938.

25. *Las Vegas Evening Review Journal,* March 26, 1940; *Nevada State Journal,* July 26, 1940.

26. *Las Vegas Age,* December 13, 1940.

27. *Las Vegas Evening Review Journal,* April 14, 1941.

28. *Las Vegas Evening Review Journal,* December 13, 1938.

29. Buck Brush Spring Development file.

30. *Las Vegas Age,* December 13, 1940.

8 | Building Playgrounds in the Desert: The National Park Service and the CCC

1. Elliott, *History of Nevada,* 264, 274–75.

2. *Nevada State Parks System Plan.*

3. Linda Flint McClellan, *Presenting Nature: The Historic Landscape Design of the National Park Service, 1916 to 1942.*

4. John C. Paige, *The Civilian Conservation Corps and the National Park Service, 1933–1942: An Administrative History.*

5. *Nevada State Parks System Plan,* 1–7; James G. Scrugham to Thomas Woodnut Miller, December 12, 1933, Miller Papers.

6. *Reno Evening Gazette,* March 7, 1939; "Park Service to Assist at Lake Mead."

7. Arno B. Cammerer, "Building a Playground at Boulder Beach," 222.

8. Ibid.

9. "March Report of Superintendent Guy D. Edwards, Nevada State Parks Camps, SP-4 and SP-6 at Boulder City, Nevada."

10. Ibid., 223; "March Report of Superintendent C. M. Bailey, Under Supervision of the National Park Service, in Cooperation with the Bureau of Reclamation, SP-6, Boulder City."

11. "March Report of Superintendent Guy D. Edwards."

12. Ibid.

13. Cammerer, “Building a Playground”; Frank Wright, “Desert Airways: A Short History of Clark County Aviation, 1920–1948,” 13.

14. Louis Schellbach, “The Lost City of Nevada.”

15. M. R. Harrington, “The Lost City of Nevada—a Few Facts,” 90; Albert H. Schroeder, “The Archeological Excavations at Willow Beach, Arizona, 1950,” 63–71; Lysenda Kirkberg, *The Lost City: An Original Documentary Teleplay.*

16. E. H. Heinemann, “Lake Mead Disturbs the Ancient Indian.”

17. Charles E. Guy, interview by Dennis McBride, 1995, Boulder City Library Oral History Project, Boulder City (Nev.) Library.

18. *Caliente Herald,* August 10, 1933; April 19, 1934; *Nevada State Journal,* February 15, 1935.

19. *Caliente Herald,* December 13, 1934; *Ely Daily Times,* October 7, 1933.

20. See Nevada Writers' Project of the Works Projects Administration, *The WPA Guide to 1930s Nevada.*

21. Harold Housley, “Notes and Documents: Elwood Decker and the CCC at Fort Churchill”; Robert Erwood, “Camp Notes.”

22. *Nevada State Journal,* February 5, 1935; July 7, 1936; *Las Vegas Review Journal,* February 12, 1934.

23. Christine E. Savage, *New Deal Adobe: The Civilian Conservation Corps and the Reconstruction of Mission La Purisima, 1934–1942,* 68.

24. Housley, “Notes and Documents,” 109, 111–13.

25. *Reno Gazette Journal,* August 25, 1996; Elwood Decker, “Letters.”

26. Raymond Fry, interview by Victoria Ford, October 25, 2000, University of Nevada Oral Historic Program, Reno.

27. *Las Vegas Evening Review Journal,* January 11, January 25, 1937; *Ely Daily Times,* January 25, 1937.

28. Mary Ellen Glass, *Nevada's Turbulent '50s: Decade of Political and Economic Change.*

9 | Military Expansion in Hawthorne: The Navy and the CCC

1. DOD Explosives Safety Board (DDESB), http://www.acq.osd.mil/ens/esb.esbhompb.htlm.

2. “History of Water Development.”

3. H. S. Babbitt to Patrick A. McCarran, August 6, 1936, McCarran Papers.

4. Ibid.

5. *Mineral County Independent,* September 20, 1933.

6. *Mineral County Independent,* August 2, 1933.

7. *Reno Evening Gazette,* June 25, 1935.

8. *Ely Daily Times,* September 28, 1936.

9. *Mineral County Independent,* November 14, 1934.

10. Babbitt to McCarran, August 6, 1936, McCarran Papers.

11. McCarran to staff member, n.d., McCarran Papers.

12. *Mineral County Independent and Hawthorne News,* May 19, 1937.

13. "Official Annual."

14. *Mineral County Independent,* August 2, 1933.

15. *Mineral County Independent,* May 30, 1934.

16. Babbitt to regional forester (San Francisco), February 4, 1936, McCarran Papers.

17. M. J. Bowen to Robert Fechner, July 15, 1937, NARA, FSA, CCC, Record Group 35, entry 115, Camp Inspection Reports, Nevada, Camp Hawthorne.

18. Waller H. Reed, "Population of Nevada Counties and Communities, 1860–1980."

19. James C. Reddoch to Robert Fechner, March 1935, NARA, CCC, Record Group 35, entry 115, Camp Inspection Reports, Nevada, Camp Hawthorne.

20. Bowen to Fechner, July 15, 1937, ibid.

21. William H. Callahan to Glen D. Reese, August 10, 1937, ibid.

22. W. Frank Persons to J. J. McEntee, September 2, 1937, ibid.; *Mineral County Independent and Hawthorne News,* July 14, 1937.

23. *Mineral County Independent and Hawthorne News,* July 13, 1938.

24. *Mineral County Independent and Hawthorne News,* November 23, 1938.

25. Crawford interview.

10 | Building Ranger Stations and Mountain Parks: The National Forest Service's CCC Program

1. Richa Wilson, "Privies, Pastures, and Portables: Administrative Facilities of the Humboldt-Toiyabe National Forest, 1891–1950."

2. Jane Pieplow, "Historical Significance for Humboldt Forest CCC-Built Administrative Sites."

3. Wilson, "Privies, Pastures, and Portables."

4. H. R. Kylie, G. H. Hieronymus, and A. G. Hall, *CCC Forestry,* 303.

5. Otis and others, "Forest Service."

6. *Eureka Sentinel,* June 13, 1936.

7. Wilson, "Privies, Pastures, and Portables," 190–98.

8. Pieplow, "Historical Significance."

9. *Ely Daily Times,* June 1, 1933.

10. *Las Vegas Evening Review Journal,* May 5, 1933.

11. *Happy Days,* September 22, 1934.

12. M. J. Bowen to Robert Fechner, August 27, 1936, NARA, CCC, Record Group 35, entry 115, Camp Inspection Reports, Nevada, Camp Lamoille.

13. *Ely Daily Times,* September 6, 1933.

14. *Ely Daily Times,* August 23, 1933.

15. *Ely Daily Times,* September 1, 1933.

16. *Ely Daily Times,* July 25, 1933.

17. *Ely Daily Times,* March 12, 1936; *Ely Record,* October, 23, 1936.

18. *Ely Daily Times,* October 19, 1933.

19. *Reno Evening Gazette,* January 19, 1938.

20. *Pictorial Review.*

21. *Elko Free Press,* June 8, 1940.

22. Fred Frampton, "Indian Creek Bridge Replacement: Humboldt Toiyabe National Forest Cultural Resource Report, HM-98-0789."

23. *Humboldt Star,* August 6, 1935.

24. Wilson, "Privies, Pastures, and Portables."

25. *Humboldt Hummer,* September 5, 1936.

26. Bowen to Fechner, February 20, 1937, NARA, CCC, Record Group 35, entry 115, Camp Inspection Report, Nevada, Camp Reese River.

27. *Tonopah Times Bonanza,* July 22, 1939.

28. *Reno Evening Gazette,* April 11, 1936.

29. E. S. Adams to J. J. McEntee, November 21, 1941, NARA, FSA, CCC, Record Group 35, entry 115, Camp Inspection Report, Nevada, Camp Reese River; Fremont B. Houson to the director of the Civilian Conservation Corps, January 28, 1941, ibid., Camp Paradise.

30. Bowen to Fechner, July 30, 1937, ibid., Camp Charleston Mountain.

31. A. W. Stockman to the director of the Civilian Conservation Corps, August 31, 1938, "Camp Inspection Supplemental Report," ibid.

32. Otis and others, "Forest Service," 37.

33. *Las Vegas Evening Review Journal,* October 1, 1935; Kathy Moskowitz, "A Prehistory and History of the Spring Mountains National Recreation Area."

34. *Ely Daily Times,* June 11, 1937; Stockman to the director of the Civilian Conservation Corps, August 19, 1939, "Camp Inspection Supplemental Report," NARA, CCC, Record Group 35, entry 115, Camp Inspection Reports, Nevada, Camp Charleston Mountain.

35. Paul Lytle, interview by Dennis McBride, June 12, 1995, Boulder City Oral History Project, Boulder City (Nev.) Library.

36. *Las Vegas Evening Review Journal,* July 13, 1937.

37. Bowen to the director of the Civilian Conservation Corps, June 10, 1942, Camp Inspection Report, NARA, FSA, CCC, Record Group 35, entry 115, Camp Charleston Mountain.

38. Wilson, "Privies, Pastures, and Portables."

39. *Reno Evening Gazette,* March 21, 1940.

40. Fred Frampton, conversation with Renée Corona Kolvet, September 12, 2003.

41. *Nevada State Journal,* November 8, 1940, November 23, 1941.

42. *Reno Evening Gazette,* August 13, 1940.

43. City of Reno employee Joe Teixeira, telephone conversation with Renée Corona Kolvet, November 10, 2003.

44. *Reno Evening Gazette,* August 13, 1940; *Nevada State Journal,* November 23, 1941.

45. *Record Courier,* June 5, 1942.

46. As an enrollee at Camp Paradise, Mr. Rosowski sometimes babysat the Timmons children. Decades later, around 1995, Mr. Rosowski and his wife, Alma, drove from Batavia, New York, to Midas, Nevada, to visit Wilbur and Edna Timmons.

47. While at Camp Paradise, Mr. Rosowski had an allergic reaction to the shot for Rocky Mountain spotted fever, and Dr. Anderson saved his life by giving him a shot of adrenalin in the chest.

48. Edmund Rosowski, interview by Victoria Ford, September 30, 2000, University of Nevada Oral History Program, Reno.

11 | Controlling Erosion along Nevada Waterways: The CCC and the Soil Conservation Service

1. D. J. Johnson, "Meadow Valley Wash Watershed," NRCS, Caliente, n.d.

2. Hugh Shamberger, "State of Nevada, Report on the Muddy River, Clark County Nevada," Hugh Shamberger Papers, 21.

3. Louie A. Gardella, *Just Passing Through: My Work in Nevada Agriculture, Agricultural Extension, and Western Water Resources,* 108.

4. Ibid.

5. Shamberger, "State of Nevada," 26, 23.

6. "A Story of Land and People," http://www.nrcs.usda.gov/about/history, May 26, 2002.

7. *Record Courier,* August 15, 1941.

8. Address of Robert Fechner, director of ECW, May 6, 1933, Official File 268, Civilian Conservation Corps, FDR Library, 12.

9. *Ely Daily Times,* March 25, 1936.

10. Jim Griswold, "Report on Flood in Meadow Valley Wash, March 3rd to 5th Inclusive," March 12, 1938, Jim Griswold Papers.

11. Gardella, *Just Passing Through,* 71–73.

12. *Caliente Herald,* November 22, 1934; Corey Lytle, conversation with Renée Corona Kolvet, June 16, 2003.

13. Leo Stewart, telephone conversation with Renée Corona Kolvet, August 24, 2003; Cleo Connell, telephone conversation with Renée Corona Kolvet, August 23, 2003.

14. Joe Higbee, telephone conversation with Renée Corona Kolvet, August 22, 2003.

15. *Caliente Herald,* March 29, 1934.

16. "Tile Drains."

17. Shamberger, "State of Nevada," 22.

18. Jarrod Edmonds, conversation with Renée Corona Kolvet, September 15, 2003; Bill Singleton, "Feasibility Assessment and Design Estimate for Moapa Dams, Moapa Indian Reservation, Clark County, Nevada."

19. Shamberger, "State of Nevada," 23.

20. Arabell Lee Hafner, *100 Years on the Muddy,* 249.

21. "Moapa Valley Pumping Project Feasibility Report," C-3.

22. Cecil W. Creel to J. H. Wittwer, October 18, 1940, Humboldt-Toiyabe National Forest Office, Elko.

23. Patrick McCarran to Edwin Marshall, October 19, 1940, ibid.

24. *Ely Daily Times,* March 25, 1936.

25. Gary Hafen, conversation with Renée Corona Kolvet, August 27, 2003; John Lewis Pulsipher, *The Life and Travels of John Lewis Pulsipher, 1884–1963: The Autobiography of a Southern Nevada Pioneer.*

26. *Ely Daily Times,* March 25, 1936.

27. Charles D. Jarrett, "Looking around Bunkerville." NARA, Pacific Sierra Region, Records of the Soil Conservation Service, Region 10, Record Group 114, General Records, Caliente Area Office, 1935–1942.

28. "Safety Meeting Minutes," March 9, 1937. Camp Bunkerville, Company 4791, NARA, Pacific Sierra Region, Records of the Soil Conservation Service, Region 10, Record Group 114, General Records, Caliente Area Office, 1935–1942.

29. Michael Johnson, telephone conversation with Renée Corona Kolvet, September 2, 2003.

30. "History and Biography of Heber Herbert Hardy and Betsy Leavitt Hardy."

31. Sharrell D. Williams, "A Historical Study of the Growth of the L.D.S. Church in Clark County," 74.

32. Rick Orr, conversation with Renée Corona Kolvet, August 10, 2003.

33. Lytle conversation.

34. Randall interview. Despite Mr. Randall's gruff demeanor, his students loved him. Many remained in touch with him over the years.

12 | The CCC Legacy in Nevada

1. Salmond, *Civilian Conservation Corps,* 127.

2. William D. Rowley, *U.S. Forest Service Grazing and Rangelands,* 173.

3. Hal K. Rothman, *Saving the Planet: The American Response to the Environment in the Twentieth Century,* 87.

4. Fulwider, "Resource Management to People Management," 25.

5. Austin Childs to Maurice P. Molyneaux, October 31, 1991, Mineral County Museum, Hawthorne.

6. "Thanksgiving Program," Company 4743, Camp Newlands, 1936, now in the possession of former enrollee Ralph Hash.

7. *Record Courier,* November 4, 1938.

8. Wilbur interview.

9. Alfred E. Golze, "Reclamation Trains the CCC Enrollee."

10. Michael DeCarlo, interview by Victoria Ford, October 3, 2000, University of Nevada Oral History Program, Reno.

11. Smith, "New Deal Relief Programs."

12. Edna Timmons, telephone conversation with Renée Corona Kolvet, July 1, 1999.

13. *Humboldt Star,* July 31, 1939.

14. Rosowski interview.

15. *Record Courier,* February 7, 1941.

16. *Ely Daily Times,* January 12, 1937.

17. *Elko Free Press,* July 31, 1990.

18. "Senate Resolution 207 Declared March 31 as National CCC Day."

BIBLIOGRAPHY

Manuscript Collections

Decker, Elwood. "Letters." Civilian Conservation Corps Files. Nevada Historical Society, Reno.

Erwood, Robert. "Camp Notes." National Association for Civilian Conservation Corps Alumni, St. Louis, Mo.

Griswold, Jim. Papers. University of Nevada–Reno Library.

McCarran, Patrick A., Papers. Nevada Historical Society, Reno.

Miller, Thomas Woodnut. Papers. University of Nevada–Reno Library.

Shamberger, Hugh. Papers. University of Nevada–Reno Library.

Washoe County Water Conservation District. Correspondence. Nevada Historical Society, Reno.

Government Documents

"Address of Robert Fechner, Director of ECW, May 6, 1933." Official file 268, Civilian Conservation Corp, 12. Franklin D. Roosevelt Library, National Archives, Washington, D.C.

"A Brief Summary of Certain Phases of the Civilian Conservation Corps (Alaska through Wyoming and the United States), April 1933–June 30, 1938." Record Group 35, entry 46, Statistic Reports on Enrollees, Nevada. Records of the Civilian Conservation Corps, National Archives, College Park, Md.

"A Brief Summary of Certain Phases of the Civilian Conservation Corps (Alaska through Wyoming and the United States), 1942." Record Group 35, entry 46, Statistic Reports on Enrollees, Nevada. Civilian Conservation Corps, National Archives, College Park, Md.

Bustard, Bruce. *A New Deal for the Arts.* Washington, D.C.: National Archives, 1997.

"Directory of the Civilian Conservation Corps Camps, Tenth Period, 1937–1938." Official file 268, Civilian Conservation Corps. Franklin D. Roosevelt Library, National Archives, Washington, D.C.

DOD Explosives Safety Board. http://www.acq.osd.mil/ens/esb.esbhompb.htlm.

DOL. "Age Distribution of Juniors Enrolled in the Civilian Conservation Corps during the June–August Enrollment, 1935." Record Group 35, entry 46, Statistical Reports on Enrollees, Nevada. Records of the Civilian Conservation Corps, National Archives, College Park, Md.

———. "Age Distribution of 238,846 Juniors Selected and Accepted for the Civilian Conservation Corps, October 1–November 15, 1935, April 1–15, 1936, and July 1–31, 1936." Record Group 35, entry 46, Statistical Reports on Enrollees, Nevada. Records of the Civilian Conservation Corps, National Archives, College Park, Md.

———. "Fiscal Year Report for CCC Activities for Year Ended June 30, 1937." Record Group 35, entry 46, Statistical Reports on Enrollees, Nevada. Records of the Civilian Conservation Corps, National Archives, College Park, Md.

———. "Height of Juniors Accepted for Enrollment, January 1940; Weight of Juniors Accepted for Enrollment, January 1940." Record Group 35, entry 46, Statistical Reports on Enrollees, Nevada. Records of the Civilian Conservation Corps, National Archives, College Park, Md.

———. "Summary of CCC Statistical Data for Nevada, January 6, 1939." Record Group 35, entry 46, Statistical Reports on Enrollees, Utah. Records of the Civilian Conservation Corps, National Archives, College Park, Md.

———. "Summary of CCC Statistical Data for Nevada, July 22, 1939." NARA, FSA, CCC, Record Group 35, entry 46, Statistical Reports on Enrollees, Nevada. Records of the Civilian Conservation Corps, National Archives, College Park, Md.

Herndon, Paul. *The Taylor Grazing Act: History of Grazing on Public Lands.* N.p.: USDI, Bureau of Land Management, 1984.

"Instructions Governing the Selection of Veterans to Compose the Veterans Contingent of the Civilian Conservation Corps, Supplement no. 2 to Instructions of September 7, 1937." Veterans Administration. Record Group 35, entry 46, Statistical Reports on Enrollees, Nevada. Records of the Civilian Conservation Corps, National Archives, College Park, Md.

Jarrett, Charles D. "Looking around Bunkerville." *Western Farm and Home Hour,* April 19, 1937. Record Group 114, Records of Soil Conservation Service, Pacific Southwest Region, General Records, 1935–1942, Caliente, Nev. National Archives, Pacific Sierra Region, San Bruno, Calif.

Kylie, H. R., G. H. Hieronymus, and A. G. Hall, *CCC Forestry.* Washington, D.C.: U.S. Government Printing Office, 1937.

Linenberger, Toni Rae. *Dams, Dynamos, and Development: The Bureau of Reclamation's Power Program and Electification of the West.* Denver: USDI, 2002.

McClellan, Linda Flint. *Presenting Nature: The Historic Landscape Design of the National Park Service, 1916 to 1942.* Washington, D.C.: USDI, National Park Service, 1993.

"Monthly Statistical Summaries for July and September 1941." Record Group 35, entry 49, Monthly Reports on Enrollment, Nevada. Records of the Civilian Conservation Corps, National Archives, College Park, Md.

Muhn, James, and Hanson R. Stuart. *Opportunity and Challenge: The Story of the BLM.* N.p.: USDI, Bureau of Land Management, 1988.

Paige, John C. *The Civilian Conservation Corps and the National Park Service, 1933–1942: An Administrative History.* N.p.: USDI, National Park Service, 1985.

"Safety Meeting Minutes." March 9, 1937, Camp Bunkerville, Company 4791. Record Group 114, Records of the Soil Conservation Service, Region 10, General Records, 1935–1942. Caliente, Nev. National Archives, Pacific Sierra Region, San Bruno, Calif.

"Statement of Robert Fechner to the U.S. Senate Special Committee to Investigate Unemployment, March 15, 1938." Official file 268, Civilian Conservation Corps. Franklin D. Roosevelt Library, National Archives, Washington, D.C.

Taylor, Edward T. "American Democracy on the Range." *Congressional Record Appendix* (July 1, 1940), 13753.

"Urban-Rural Classifications of Juniors Accepted for Enrollment in the Civilian Conservation Corps, January, 1941." FSA, CCC, Record Group 35, entry 46, Statistical Reports on Enrollees, Nevada. Records of the Civilian Conservation Corps, National Archives, College Park, Md.

"Years of Schooling Completed by Junior Enrollees in January 1940 and October 1940." FSA, CCC, Record Group 35, entry 46, Statistical Reports on Enrollees, Nevada. Records of the Civilian Conservation Corps, National Archives, College Park, Md.

Your CCC: A Handbook for Enrollees. Washington, D.C.: Happy Days Publishing, n.d.

Unpublished Government Documents

USDA

Frampton, Fred. "Indian Creek Bridge Replacement: Humboldt-Toiyabe National Forest Cultural Resource Report, HM-98-0789." June 26, 1998.

Otis, Alison T., William D. Honey, Thomas C. Hogg, and Kimberly K. Lakin. "The Forest Service and the Civilian Conservation Corps, 1933–1942." USDA, Forest Service, August 1986.

Pieplow, Jane. "Historical Significance for Humboldt Forest CCC-Built Administrative Sites." Mountain City Ranger District Office, Elko.

"Report on Wells Siding–Bowman Reservoir Project, Work Done by CCC Company 538, Camp PE 206, Under Direction of the United States Forest Service, Spring Fall, 1934/35." Humboldt-Toiyabe National Forest, Elko.

"A Story of Land and People." May 26, 2002. http://www.nrcs.usda.gov/about/history.

"Tile Drains." SCS file N-3-6, Pahranagat Valley SCD, 1942.

Wilson, Richa. "Privies, Pastures, and Portables: Administrative Facilities of the Humboldt-Toiyabe National Forest, 1891–1950." November 2000.

USDI

Buck Brush Spring Development file, Bureau of Land Management, Carson City Field Office.

Desert National Wildlife Range, pamphlet, U.S. Fish and Wildlife Service, June 2000.

McGuckian, Peggy. "Report Commemorating 50 Years of the Taylor Grazing Act, Bureau of Land Management." Winnemucca Field Office, 1984.

"Moapa Valley Pumping Project Feasibility Report." Bureau of Reclamation, June 1970.

NPS. "March Report of Superintendent Guy D. Edwards, Nevada State Parks Camps, SP-4 and SP-6 at Boulder City, Nevada." April 1, 1936.

———. "March Report of Superintendent C. M. Bailey, Under Supervision of the National Parks Service in Cooperation with the Bureau of Reclamation, SP-6, Boulder City." April 1, 1936.

Pfaff, Christine, "The Bureau of Reclamation and the Civilian Conservation Corps, 1933–1942." USDI, Bureau of Reclamation, June 2000.

"Project Application, Project no. 525, Camp 87, Region 3." USDI Bureau of Land Management, Carson City Field Office, 1939.

"Quarterly Narrative Report, May 8 through June 30, 1940." Ruby Lake Camp FWS-3, Wells, Nev. USDI.

"Quarterly Narrative Report, July through September 1940." Ruby Lake Camp FWS-3, Wells, Nev. USDI.

"Quarterly Narrative Report for Months of July, August, and September [1941]." Ruby Lake Camp FWS-3, Wells, Nev. USDI.

"Quarterly Narrative Report for the Months of October, November, December 1941 and January, February, March and April, 1942 to May 15, 1942." Ruby Lake Camp FWS-3, Wells, Nev. USDI.

Singleton, Bill. "Feasibility Assessment and Design Estimate for Moapa Dams, Moapa Indian Reservation, Clark County, Nevada." Bureau of Reclamation, USDI, February 2000.

"Short History of the Refuge System, Organization and Growth (1921–1955)." http://www.refuge.fws.gov.

Speulda, Lou Ann. "Evaluation and Assessment Report for the Virgin Valley Campground Bath House, Sheldon NWR, Humboldt County, Nevada, 5 October 1995." USDI.

Newspapers and Miscellaneous

Camp Newlands (Company 4743) Thanksgiving Program, courtesy of Ralph Hash
Caliente Herald
Camp Newlands Courier (Fallon)
Carson City Appeal
Elko Free Press
Elko Independent
Ely Daily Times
Ely Record
Eureka Sentinel
Fallon Standard
Humboldt Hummer
Humboldt Star (Winnemucca)
Las Vegas Age
Las Vegas Evening Review Journal
Mineral County Independent (Hawthorne)
Mineral County Independent and Hawthorne News (Hawthorne)
Nevada State Journal (Reno)
New York Times
Record Courier (Gardnerville)
Reno Evening Gazette
Sacramento Bee
Tonopah Daily Times

Other Sources

Alcorn, J. R. "Life History Notes on the Piute Ground Squirrel." *Journal of Mammology* (May 1940).

Bureau of Reclamation. *Annual Project History, Humboldt Project, 1934, 1935, 1936.* Denver: NARA.

Arrington, Leonard. "The New Deal in the West: A Preliminary Statistical Inquiry." *Pacific Historical Review* 38, no. 3 (1969): 314–16.

Cammerer, Arno B. "Building a Playground at Boulder Beach." *Reclamation Era* (November 1938): 222–24.

Cole, Olen, Jr. *The African-American Experience in the Civilian Conservation Corps.* Gainesville: University Press of Florida, 1999.

Couch, Jim F., and William F. Shughart II. *The Political Economy of the New Deal.* Cheltenham, Eng., and Northampton, Mass.: Locke Institute, 1998.

Dallas, Harry. "An Army for Land Conservation Work." *NACCCA Journal* 22, no. 10 (October 1999).

Edwards, Jerome E. "Nevada Power Broker: Pat McCarran and His Political Machine." In *Nevada Readings and Perspectives,* edited by Michael S. Green and Gary E. Elliot. Reno: Nevada Historical Society, 1997.

———. *Pat McCarran: Political Boss of Nevada.* Reno: University of Nevada Press, 1982.

Elliott, Russell R. *Growing Up in a Company Town.* Reno: Nevada Historical Society, 1990.

———. *History of Nevada.* Lincoln: University of Nebraska Press, 1973.

Freidel, Frank. *Franklin D. Roosevelt: A Rendezvous with Destiny.* Boston: Little, Brown, 1990.

———. *Franklin D. Roosevelt: Launching the New Deal.* Boston: Little, Brown, 1973.

Fulwider, Derrel S. "From Resource Management to People Management: Reflections of a Federal Land Manager." *North Central Nevada Historical Society Quarterly* (Winter–Spring 1986).

Gardella, Louie A. *Just Passing Through: My Work in Nevada Agriculture, Agricultural Extension, and Western Water Resources.* Reno: University of Nevada, Reno Library, Oral History Project, 1975.

Glad, Betty. *Key Pittman: The Tragedy of a Senate Insider.* New York: Columbia University Press, 1986.

Glass, Mary Ellen. *Nevada's Turbulent '50s: Decade of Political and Economic Change.* Reno: University of Nevada Press, 1981.

Golze, Alfred E. "Reclamation Trains the CCC Enrollee." *Reclamation Era* (March 1939).

Green, Michael S., and Gary E. Elliott. "Gaming and Tourism." In *Nevada Readings and Perspectives,* edited by Michael S. Green and Gary E. Elliott. Reno: Nevada Historical Society, 1997.

Hafner, Arabell Lee. *100 Years on the Muddy.* Springville, Utah: Art City Publishing, 1967.

Harrington, M. R. "The Lost City of Nevada—a Few Facts." *Reclamation Era* (May 1935): 90–91.

Heinemann, E. H. "Lake Mead Disturbs the Ancient Indian." *Reclamation Era* (August 1936): 180–83.

"Historical Sketch of the Sacramento District CCC and Pictorial Review of Company 1212." Camp Paradise, 1940.

"History and Biography of Heber Herbert Hardy and Betsy Leavitt Hardy." On file at the Virgin Valley Heritage Museum, Mesquite, Nev.

"History of Water Development." Naval Ammunition Depot, Hawthorne, Nev.

Housley, Harold. "Notes and Documents: Elwood Decker and the CCC at Fort Churchill." *Nevada Historical Society Quarterly* (Summer 1995).

Hulse, James W. *Forty Years in the Wilderness: Impressions of Nevada, 1940–1980.* Reno: University of Nevada Press, 1986.

Humboldt Hummer. Elko, Nev. September 5, 1936.

Jackson, Donald Dale. "They Were Poor, Hungry, and They Built to Last." *Smithsonian* 25, no. 9 (December 1994): 66–77.

Kennedy, David M. *Freedom from Fear: The American People in Depression and War, 1929–1945.* New York: Oxford University Press, 1999.

Kirkberg, Lysenda. *The Lost City: An Original Documentary Teleplay.* Boulder City, Nev.: Lake Mead National Recreation Area, 1984.

Kolvet, Renée Corona. *A New Deal in the Desert: Civilian Conservation Corps in Nevada, Mapping Project.* Reno: Bureau of Land Management, 2001.

Lowitt, Richard, and Maurine Beasley, eds. *One-third of a Nation: Lorena Hickok Reports on the Great Depression.* Chicago: University of Illinois Press, 2000.

Moehring, Eugene P. "The Federal Trigger." In *Nevada Readings and Perspectives,* edited by Michael S. Green and Gary E. Elliott. Reno: Nevada Historical Society, 1997.

Moskowitz, Kathy. "A Prehistory and History of the Spring Mountains National Recreation Area." On file at the Spring Mountains National Recreation Area in Las Vegas.

Murchie, Archie. *The Free Life of a Ranger, 1929–1965.* Reno: University of Nevada Oral History Program, 1991.

Murphy, Ralph. "Sheldon National Wildlife Refuge: A Collection of Historical Vignettes." On file at the U.S. Fish and Wildlife Service's state office in Reno.

Nevada State Parks System Plan. Carson City: Nevada State Park System, 1997.

Nevada Writers' Project of the Works Projects Administration. *The WPA Guide to 1930s Nevada.* Reno: University of Nevada Press, 1991.

"Official Annual." Civilian Conservation Corps, Sacramento District, Ninth Corps Area, 1938.

"Park Service to Assist at Lake Mead." *Reclamation Era* (March 1936): 65.

Persons, W. Frank. "Selecting 1,800,000 Young Men for the C.C.C." *Monthly Labor Review* (April 1938).

Pictorial Review. Civilian Conservation Corps, Sacramento District, Company 1212, Camp Paradise, 1940.

Pieplow, Jane. "Government Programs Come to Fallon and Churchill County, Civilian Conservation Corps." *Churchill County in Focus* (Churchill County Museum Association) (1999–2000): 80–81.

Pruitt, Tim. "Cricket Gangs." *Northeastern Nevada Historical Society Quarterly* (Summer 1978): 114–16.

Pulsipher, John Lewis. *The Life and Travels of John Lewis Pulsipher, 1884–1963: The Autobiography of a Southern Nevada Pioneer.* Salt Lake City: V. O. Young, 1970.

Raymond, C. Elizabeth. *George Wingfield: Owner and Operator of Nevada.* Reno: University of Nevada Press, 1992.

Reading, Don C. "A Statistical Analysis of New Deal Economic Programs in the Forty-eight States." Ph.D diss., Utah State University, 1972.

Reed, Waller H. "Population of Nevada Counties and Communities, 1860–1980." On file at the Nevada Historical Society, Reno, 1984.

"Roosevelt's Tree Army: A Brief History of the Civilian Conservation Corps." http://www.cccalumni.org/history1/html.

Rothman, Hal K. *Saving the Planet: The American Response to the Environment in the Twentieth Century.* Chicago: Ivan R. Dee, 2000.

Rowley, William D. *U.S. Forest Service Grazing and Rangelands.* College Station: Texas A&M Press, 1985.

Salmond, John A. *The Civilian Conservation Corps, 1933–1942: A New Deal Case Study.* Durham, N.C.: Duke University Press, 1967.

Savage, Christine E. *New Deal Adobe: The Civilian Conservation Corps and the Reconstruction of Mission La Purisima, 1934–1942.* Santa Barbara: Fifian Press, 1991.

Schellbach, Louis. "The Lost City of Nevada." *Arrowhead Magazine* (December 1924).

Schroeder, Albert H. "The Archeological Excavations at Willow Beach, Arizona, 1950." *University of Utah Anthropological Papers* 50 (April 1961).

Schweikart, Larry. "A New Perspective on George Wingfield and Nevada Banking, 1920–1933." In *Money and Banking: The American Experience.* Fairfax, Va.: George Mason University Press, 1995.

"Senate Resolution 207 Declared March 31 as National CCC Day." *NACCCA Journal* 25, no. 3 (March 2002).

Smith, Harold Truman. "New Deal Relief Programs in Nevada, 1933 to 1935." Ph.D. diss., University of Nevada–Reno, 1972.

Thornton, C. J. *Entrepreneur: Agriculture, Business, Politics; An Oral History Conducted by Mary Ellen Glass.* Reno: University of Nevada Oral History Program, 1983.

Townley, John M. *Turn This Water into Gold: The Story of the Newlands Project.* Reno: Nevada Historical Society, 1998.

Wallis, J. J. "The Political Economy of New Deal Spending Revisited, Again: With and Without Nevada." *Explorations in Economic History* 35 (April 1998): 140–70.

Williams, Sharrell D. "A Historical Study of the Growth of the L.D.S. Church in Clark County, Nevada." Master's thesis, Brigham Young University, 1963.

Williamson, Thomas. "CCC Construction of Parapet and Curb Walls Rye Patch Dam, Humboldt Project, Nevada." *Reclamation Era* (January 1939): 15–16.

Wright, Frank. *Desert Airways: A Short History of Clark County Aviation, 1920–1948."* Occasional Paper no. 1. Las Vegas: Clark County Heritage Museum, 1993.

INDEX